# Linda in the Light

# Linda in the Light

The Incredible True Story That
Will Change Your Life Forever

Dr. Frank A. La Batto

Printed by CreateSpace.
First Edition.

ISBN-13: 978-1534937871

Cover design: Francis Bonnet
and Dr. Frank A. La Batto

Printed in the United States of America

www.lindainthelight.com

# Table of Contents

*Linda*

*My Daughter*

*My Twin Soul*


*I kept my promise*

*to write the book.*

. . . for it is in the giving that we receive,

it is in the pardoning that we are pardoned,

and it is in dying that we are born to eternal life.

– *THE PRAYER OF ST. FRANCIS*

*True love, pure unconditional love, transcends time and space. Knowing no time or space on the other side allows for everything on all planes of existence to happen simultaneously in the now.*

DR. FRANK A. LA BATTO

*Transition is the lifting of the veil between the physical and non-physical, the rebirth, the transfiguration of the soul in the light.*

DR. FRANK A. LA BATTO

# A True Story

I present to you *Linda in the Light,* a memoir written by a father honoring the request of his daughter after she transitions into the light of eternal life; a transition we will all experience.

What lies ahead is a glorious and true journey of angels, healers, and guides. Everything is real. Everything is normal. Any fear of death will be erased for we are the lucky ones. We have been given the opportunity to examine our lives, to change our courses, to alter our destinies, because our children, our teachers, via their transitions, have courageously fulfilled the promises they made before they were born, allowing us to learn, grow, and love. We cannot let them down. We are their parents. We have experienced the ultimate unimaginable tragedy of loss, separation, sorrow, pain, grief, loneliness, and despair; our hearts broken beyond repair.

But they have given their worldly lives so we can rise up into the everlasting, choosing to live beyond our materialistic attachments, and by doing so detach ourselves from the cycle of earthly incarnations just as they have.

We honor their courage through our living, laughing, and loving. Our children, by their transformations, lift the mask between the physical and non-physical, allowing us to experience eternity as an undeniable, normal, natural, essential birthright.

It is through this memoir that I introduce Linda's earthly sojourn, my earthly sojourn, and the ensuing intertwining of our journeys simultaneously in the physical and non-physical, bound by pure unconditional love.

I approach this magnificent gift as a person blessed with no special talents or abilities, just a curiosity and desire to learn how; an ability we all possess and are readily capable of mastering, no matter what prior experiences we may or may not have.

I take you through a simplified, easily-navigated knowing, an essential birthright available to all, by relating my life experiences, Linda's life experiences in both the physical and non-physical, books I have read, people I have met; expounding unequivocal, common, daily, reproducible encounters, the uninterruption of existence, the verifiability of immortality, and the fact that there is no separation, just a shift from one embodiment to the next.

There is no special formula or unique path, no near-death or profound religious experience necessary in order to lift the veil between the physical and non-physical and reconnect with our children and loved ones. This true story, this road, this journey of mine and Linda's, is one of an infinite number of journeys, something I express many times throughout the book.

*Linda in the Light* goes beyond giving hope, healing, and closure to the millions of us who have lost children or loved ones no matter what the cause of their transition. It brings reality–real, normal, everyday communication, enlightenment, a conscious awakening, and a dawning of a new way of thinking, acting, and viewing this finite world we inhabit.

It frees our souls, our inner beings to touch what is truly real–pure unconditional love–for ourselves, our children, our loved ones, and our brothers and sisters who inhabit this planet with us.

I introduce freedom to all through concrete, reproducible, verifiable experiences, opening all to the gifts our children and loved ones have given us. They are our teachers, courageously fulfilling their mission to be our guides and healers. Spirituality–not religion–facts, not fiction, are what we are here to experience.

As you will see, Linda presents herself to me in the now as our journeys interweave, and I share these experiences and knowing with all. I include time, dates, locations, and real events to bring her to you.

She communicates with me through my five senses; sight, sound, taste, smell, touch, but also through my heart, my thoughts, my emotions, humor, music, objects, lights, movies, phones, messengers, healers, guides, angels, mediums, meditations, and out-of-body experiences.

Since I am not unique, I ascertain what follows will be very familiar to many of you. My words will resonate inside of you an awakening of your own individual journey, your own knowing with your children and loved ones. You shall come to realize your own training and preparation for the lifting of your veil, recognizing the gifts your children have bestowed upon you. I have no innate ability as do many of the people I introduce to you. I share what I learn through curiosity, exploration, courage, participation, and guidance from Linda. If I can do it, so can you. Simply put, if writing this book helps one person to learn how to experience their child or loved one as truly alive beyond this physical world, that life eternal is real, then my intentions have been fulfilled!

# Monday, May 7th, 2012

I sat at my desk, my patient running late, actually welcoming the reprieve of tardiness for a change. I had been totally exhausted by the long hours at the hospital after work, driving back and forth from Brooklyn to New Jersey to Long Island, living on four hours of sleep a night. Linda was finally back at her apartment, but had developed pneumonia a few days ago and was under a physician's care.

The phone rang a little after noon and it was then I heard the words no parent ever wants to hear, "She's gone," just two days after her 27th birthday, my only child, my daughter, Linda, was gone. Time came to a standstill. I couldn't breathe and I felt a vibration overcome my body. Closing my eyes, I was enveloped in a whirling, spiraling tunnel, spinning round and round, surrounded by bright iridescence, being pulled somewhere far, far away . . .

. . . AN OUT-OF-BODY EXPERIENCE (OBE) BEGINS, SOMETHING THAT HAS HAPPENED TO ME COUNTLESS TIMES BEFORE. A FORM TAKES SHAPE IN FRONT OF ME. AS I TRAVEL DEEPER I REACH OUT TO TOUCH THIS APPARITION. BUT, MUFFLED IN THE BACKGROUND A DISTANT, FAMILIAR VOICE CALLS OUT TO ME, BARELY AUDIBLE, "DR. LA BATTO, DR. LA BATTO, I CANCELLED ALL OF YOUR PATIENTS." AS I TURN TOWARDS THE VOICE, THE VISION IN FRONT OF ME DISAPPEARS AND I AM INSTANTANEOUSLY DRAWN BACK THROUGH THE

TUNNEL, HEARING A LOUD POP IN MY EARS. MY EYES OPEN . . .

♥♥♥

I don't remember driving to New Jersey or what happened during most of that day. What I did find out was that morning when Linda's friend came by to check on her, Linda's breathing was labored and she was lethargic. By the time the paramedics arrived, she was unresponsive.

At the hospital, the attending's report was that Linda had just "stopped breathing" due to the combination of being prescribed the wrong medication and her deteriorated physiological state from the pneumonia. Breaking down in hysteria, I slumped to the floor, enthralled in despair, anguish, and bereavement; crying my heart out. I would not, could not, allow myself to accept her lying cold and lifeless before my eyes. "See you tomorrow afternoon. I'll come straight to the apartment from the office. I love you. Feel better." How could these be my last words to her! I knew her years of suffering were finally at an end. I knew I had to accept it. But how do you accept such a tragedy!

I found myself driving by my former home reliving all the fun Linda and I had; passing the park where we played baseball and went sleigh riding, stopping in front of the horse farm where I would watch her ride like the wind.

Pulling up in front of her apartment in Old Bridge having no concept of time, I was everything rolled into one: peaceful, angry, in denial, sad, destroyed, numb, and lost.

I turned the key and entered, which was my daily routine during the last few weeks to check on her two Yorkshire terriers, her four cats, and straighten up. I could hardly walk into the apartment, let alone get to the couch before Cookie and Christie began barking incessantly. They were jumping up and down on my legs wanting to be picked up. I hugged them both for Linda, for me, for comfort, sensing the stillness, the emptiness, the undulation of quiet. Then the cats came 'round, rubbing my legs, purring. They all took turns licking the teardrops from my face, knowing Linda wasn't coming home. Animals are much smarter, more intuitive than people.

Very calmly, I sadly did what a parent must: contact Linda's friends to take care of the animals, call the funeral home to make arrangements, purchase flowers, cards, and an urn for her cremation, and lastly, call the restaurant to feed all who will come pay their respects to a young woman with a huge heart and a bountiful personality.

As I sat there, I looked around imagining her daily routine: getting up, feeding the dogs and cats, hurrying into the shower, driving to work, grabbing a cup of coffee on the way. I went into her bathroom; the same Beauty and the Beast towel we bought in Disney and her favorite towel from her childhood beach house days were draped over the towel rack.

Picking them up, they smelled of sweet, little Linda: the wide-eyed, carefree child, who anticipated each adventure awaiting her. I walked into her bedroom, feeling her presence. She had a couple of pictures on her nightstand. As I made her bed she remarked to me, "Use this one for the funeral."

I returned to that OBE I was called away from earlier in the day. The significance, the beauty, the majesty, the reality of an OBE is the fact that you are experiencing everything as if you are in the present moment. All manners of touch, taste, sight, sound, environment, emotion, feeling, action, and thought are real as in the conscious state, equal to taking a cold shower in the morning . . .

. . . LINDA IS LYING ON HER BED, PEACEFUL, HAPPY, GLOWING, AND ANTICIPATING MY ARRIVAL. KNEELING NEXT TO HER, SHE IS FAST ASLEEP. I KISS HER FOREHEAD, THEN HER LIPS, HER SKIN PINK AND SOFT. THE FAMILIARITY OF HER TOUCH RUSHES THROUGH MY

BODY. I FEEL THE SAME ELATION AND BLISS AS IF IT WERE THE FIRST TIME HOLDING HER AS A NEWBORN, GAZING INTO HER CAPTIVATING, ENCHANTING, ANGELIC FACE. SHE IS IN A LONG-SLEEVE WHITE GOWN WITH A RUFFLED COLLAR, TUCKED TENDERLY UNDER A YELLOW BLANKET. THE TEARS STREAM DOWN MY CHEEKS LANDING SOFTLY, GENTLY, SLOWLY, ONTO HERS. I NOTICE HER DAINTY HANDS, HER DELICATE, BEAUTIFUL FINGERS WITH HER NAILS PAINTED IN A SOOTHING LAVENDER. I BREATHE IN THE SCENT OF HER BROWN HAIR FLOWING LAZILY IN LONG CURLS ON THE PILLOW. I CAN HEAR THE MUSICAL SOUND OF HER LAUGHTER, THE INTONATIONS IN HER VOICE. I WHISPER IN HER EAR, THE SAME EAR I GENTLY KISSED EVERY NIGHT AT BEDTIME WHEN SHE WAS A CHILD. "YOU TOLD ME TO GO HOME LAST NIGHT BECAUSE YOU SAID YOU WERE OKAY. YOU'VE BEEN THROUGH THIS NUMEROUS TIMES. I BELIEVED YOU." "TELL ME A STORY BEFORE I GO TO SLEEP," SHE WHISPERS.

I AM BROUGHT BACK TO LINDA'S BEDROOM IN MY FORMER HOME IN OLD BRIDGE. SHE IS FOUR YEARS OLD BUT DELIGHTS IN READING, RELISHING TO BE READ TO ESPECIALLY BEFORE SHE GOES TO SLEEP. "DAD," SHE INTERJECTS, "READ *SLEEPING BEAUTY*." SHE IS IN HER BLUE PAJAMAS HUGGING HER STUFFED BUNNY, THUMPER, ALONG WITH HER STUFFED CAT AND HAVE-A-HEART CARE BEAR UNDER THE COVERS. HER CHEEKS ARE GLOWING, HER LOVING BROWN EYES WIDE AND BRIGHT, HER SMILE BEAMING IN ANTICIPATION OF MY BEGINNING THE BOOK.

BUT SHE KNOWS WHAT PRECEDES, OUR BEDTIME RITUAL; THE KISSING MONSTER, THE HUGGING MONSTER, THE TICKLE MONSTER, THE NIBBLE MONSTER. THEN I TAKE MY FINGERS AND PLAY MAKEUP, GENTLY PUTTING ON EYELINER, MASCARA, FOUNDATION, BLUSH, AND LIPSTICK. "AGAIN," SHE JESTS. "YOU'RE SPOILED," I SAY. MY CHEST POUNDS WITH UNCONTROLLABLE JUBILANCE. I LOVE HER SO VERY, VERY MUCH! . . .

*Linda at four years old in her pajamas with her toy cat before bed*

Finally, at 11:00 PM that evening, I returned to my home on Long Island, sat on my living room sofa, cried my eyes out, bearing my essence to the heavens, opening up my heart to behold the torment of it broken, shattered in a million pieces, welcoming the sadness, the grief, the loneliness. I am devastated, crushed. The treasure of my vitality forever silenced. How can I go on and function following this tragedy? How can I live, stop the hurt, stop the crying? Never to hold her again in my arms. Never to talk on the phone, cook her dinner, dance with her, laugh and grieve with her. Never to walk her down the aisle, or to have the euphoria of holding a grandchild.

I cannot sleep. It is nearly 1:00 AM and I am wide awake! Linda appears facing me joyful, yet tired. Her earthly embodiment is bathed in a glow of pure radiance surrounded by a hazy green, yellow, gold, and white aura encompassing her entirely. Standing next to her are two angels, behind them the perpetual magnificence of heaven. I take a step towards her, but I can't go any further, reminded of what Jesus said to Mary Magdalene, "Do not cling to me for I have not yet ascended to the Father."

Linda enunciates, "Death is a gift, and you will write a book verifying life continues without interruption. I shall send messengers to you and you will show others what to do. You shall have documentation, third-party verification.

"When a child leaves, no matter what age, no matter what the cause, the child is the teacher, the parent is the student. The veil between the physical and non-physical is lifted by the grief process one goes through. We are free from suffering because we no longer have a body. The human form is an illusion. True love transcends time and space. You have the courage, the capacity to make the journey, to work through the heartbreak, the anguish, the despair, to complete the mission; the contract all parents and children agree to prior to embarking into mortal existence.

"But many don't understand. They do not fulfill their agreement. Anger, judgment of themselves and others, and guilt from the ego all block the miracle of the lifting of the shroud, the beauty of creation, the wonderment of the soul's journey. Our higher selves are all connected."

She smiles at me, my heart leaps for joy. Then slowly she glides away, the angels holding each of her arms. "I shall see you soon," she announces. As she moves upward I cry out, "I love you!!!"

# Linda's Journey

Linda was born on May 5th, 1985. I was in the birthing room with Linda's mother as her tiny head poked through and I counted all her little fingers and toes–elated! I held her for the first time, felt her soft, newborn skin, unspoiled and perfectly formed as I inhaled slowly, deeply, the smell, the scent of a new life, of innocence, of pure unconditional love; gazing at her tiny rosy cheeks, her cherub face, her squinting eyes.

The sounds of the physical world are strange to her. Embracing her helplessness in this new environment I am the richest, happiest person in all of creation; she's a *Mini-Me* in female form. I feel a stream of pure adulation emanating from her entering my heart, a tangible sensation of tantamount proportions, a divine, immaculate, glorified pulse of continuous rapture from this tiny infant. I couldn't contain my feet on the floor, becoming elevated, consecrated, and aware of a true, greater insight, "Life is eternal."

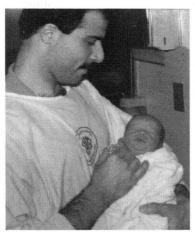

*Holding Linda on the day she is born, May 5th, 1985*

♥♥♥

For the first few months of Linda's final earthly sojourn, Linda, her mother, and I were a family. But because our journey, our road together was predetermined to be a short one, Linda's mother and I separated, and Linda was raised in two different households. We shared mutual parenting responsibilities common with divorced couples: schooling, sporting activities, social gatherings, etc.

Linda was luckier than most; being unconditionally and whole-heartily loved by two very nurturing, doting, trusting, generous, benevolent, and bestowing parents. This contributed greatly to Linda's effervescent personality; her beautiful, warm, caring soul, and the wonderful, endearing, enchanting attributes that came to define Linda.

Keep in mind because of this early separation, I can only expound Linda's journey and my journey together in both the physical and non-physical because this is what I experience with her. I am absolutely sure that the same gifts Linda bestows upon me, she equally bestows upon her mother because Linda loves us equally and completely. Their journey and knowing together is as special, and as unique, if not more so, as the journey I experience with Linda.

In one of my earliest encounters with Linda after her transition, she enlightened me with the following: "I picked you and mom to be my parents and I love you both very, very much. The journeys we chose were a courageous fulfillment honoring a commitment and an agreement we made to each other prior to our incarnations. The path was a difficult one, but one that needed to be travelled in order to fulfill each of our individual knowing and growth in the frailties and lessons of the human condition."

♥♥♥

Linda is a great soul, an old, courageous, wise soul. As a child, Linda was always very happy: giggling, laughing, smiling, and a pleasure to take to the mall or out to dinner. She didn't whine or complain and took simple delight in holding my hand or having me pick her up, run with her, or jump up and down on the bed. In turn, Linda made me jubilant. I devoted my days with her to playing games, reading books, watching movies, singing songs, and doing impersonations of her favorite characters.

She also gave of herself to others with a huge, selfless, loving heart. She spent hours beside my cousin, Jeff, who has cerebral palsy. Every Christmas, Evelyn, Jeff's mom, gave Linda a music box and she collected them until her 18th birthday. Linda's best friend was Greg, our learning disabled next door neighbor. She also befriended Clair, a beautiful young girl who lived across our court, who couldn't speak until her teenage years. Linda always brought stray cats and dogs home asking to keep them.

Whenever we had a sleepover, went on haunted hay rides, travelled to Walt Disney World, vacationed in Ocean City, Maryland, or Myrtle Beach, South Carolina, with my friends Pete, Josette, and their three delightful daughters, Christina, Regina, and Katrina, Linda spent playtime with and slept alongside Regina, their middle daughter, who has Down syndrome. The occasions with them are our most happiest. Pete and Josette have huge hearts filled with limitless affection and laughter.

Linda was a natural athlete and competitive, possessing more vitality and gusto than all the other children at school, always giving her all despite physical limitations. She was often victorious in any sport we played together, a regular tomboy. She joined a baseball team and constantly "kicked my butt" in basketball.

*Linda in her baseball uniform, 1996*

At Christmas and on her birthdays, Linda accepted every gift graciously, playing with everything she received. When old toys, dolls, stuffed animals, and games started piling up, Linda would take the pile and express, "Dad, give these to poor children. They should play with nice things too."

She enjoyed when my family came by: my sisters Connie, Terry, and Marianne, my brothers-in-law Rocky and Anthony, my cousin Roe, my father, and my two nephews and two nieces, wreaking havoc in my home. My house was the sleepover house, hide-and-go-seek-house for Linda and her friends, Ali, Lauren, and Amanda.

As a teenager, Linda was in several high school plays. She had a theatrical nature, which, along with an abounding sense of humor, made her a natural for the stage, doing impersonations of Madonna, Cher, and Streisand. Akin to yours truly, when Linda was impersonating, it came complete, incorporating mannerisms and facial expressions besides the voice. She took acting and singing lessons, going to Universal Studio's Acting School in Burbank, California for a month when she was 19.

For Linda's 16th birthday, she and my sister Terry had front row seats for a Madonna concert at the Philadelphia Spectrum. In an interview for her high school drama class, Linda played Madonna speaking about the singer's life. I have a copy of this video which I should give to Madonna at no charge, LOL.

Besides Madonna, Linda had an enormous regard for Barbra Streisand. I secured two second-row seats at Madison Square Garden in October 2006 for Linda to see Barbra Streisand in concert.

Let's not leave out Cher. Linda and I did a parody of the Sonny and Cher song, "I Got You Babe" for her high school English class. Linda had on a Cher wig, I dark glasses like Sonny. Unfortunately, I recorded over that video, but I *do* have the videotape from Linda's high school graduation party where we reprised our duet.

She also became a huge Beatles fan, and bought every Beatles CD, poster, cup, and model to match her complete Madonna, Streisand, and Cher collection!

*Linda and me as Sonny and Cher*

Linda wanted two kittens for her 18th birthday. She already had a handsome powder-blue parakeet named Pacey, whom she trained to fly from his cage to her finger to a perch on her dresser, never leaving her bedroom even with the door open all day. When Pacey stretched his wings, he displayed the spectrum of turquoise from the Mediterranean Sea off Capri to the cerulean of an impeccable summer's day in Maine.

On one of my days off, I went to several animal shelters looking to adopt kittens. My last stop was the one in my hometown of Old Bridge. As I pulled into the parking lot, Linda and her girlfriend Ali parked alongside me. I asked, "What are you doing here?" "We left school early to find kittens," Linda replied.

Simultaneously a woman pulled up on Linda's right and got out of her car with two eight-week-old kittens recently weaned. Linda peered in the carrying case and exclaimed, "These are the exact two kittens I dreamt about this morning!" "She must be psychic," I said to myself. Twenty minutes and $50 later, Linda adopted the first of her six *children*, a female tortoiseshell calico named Cleo, and a male orange tabby named Caesar.

Two years later, Linda announced she was driving to Cincinnati to buy two Yorkies, "I want sisters to keep each other company when I am in school or at work." Four days later, Christie and Cookie arrived. Feline number three, Cher, was a birthday gift from a friend when Linda turned 21. Little Kitten was rescued by Linda when she noticed her lying on the side of a road bleeding from her mouth. After nine months of rehabilitation from internal injuries, that kitten made her family complete.

At Christmas one year, Linda gave me an adorable stuffed pillow, embroidered with the following words:

> Let me get this straight,
> My *grandchild* is a dog?

She studied at Montclair College in New Jersey to become a teacher. After two years, she transferred to the College of Staten Island to study nursing. Like many young adults of her generation, she had trouble deciding on a career. To her credit, Linda gained experience in banking, communications, and retail. She landed a job with one of Verizon's franchise stores and left college to work in a field she truly liked.

Linda was charismatic. All of her cousins and friends would remark, "Linda is the coolest." When she walked into a room the atmosphere completely changed and things started to happen. Linda got invited to more parties and went on more vacations because *it just wasn't the same without her.* She enjoyed herself, had fun, and in return others enjoyed themselves too, including the adults.

Linda was filled with compassion. As she got older, she visited my elderly aunts and uncles, bringing food, ice cream, and candies, and helping with grocery shopping and household chores. In many of our videos and photos of parties and summer barbecues, Linda has her arms around the younger kids who are bored or in need of some attention. She possessed wisdom beyond her years.

She moved back home for a while in her early 20s. I observed a kind, gentle, nurturing Linda as she cared for, mothered, and fussed over her animals. Linda's exultation, her moments of bliss were when her dogs and cats were there to comfort her. Every evening, I would knock on her bedroom door to kiss her goodnight as I did when she was a little girl. Witnessing her happiness and contentment with all of her animals under the covers, reminded me of the nights when I tucked her in bed with her stuffed toys.

Linda threw me a surprise 50th birthday party, organizing the whole event, contacting all of my relatives and friends. They all commented on her outpouring of devotion and love for me; the enthusiasm, the excitement, the festivity she conveyed to everyone in planning the celebration. I was deeply honored and grateful. She made my birthday such a special and memorable one.

*Linda welcomes me at my surprise 50th birthday party*

From birth, Linda's special gift was a gregarious laugh that infected everyone around her; a healing sense of humor her greatest attribute. Linda's smile was wide, engaging, encompassing, compassionate, energizing, and contagious. She was the master of funny faces, dressing up in costumes and wigs whenever she put on a show. Her cheerfulness, lightheartedness, and optimism in the face of adversities uplifted us all. No matter how she felt, when she got ready for a party or a night out, she would always be *dressed to the nines*.

She embodied vivaciousness. Never a more beautiful, graceful, or elegant young woman was to be found anywhere! She made you feel good about yourself. Everyone called her a diva. Some of her gay guy friends made sure Linda accompanied them to the clubs in Manhattan due to her spirited ebullience, humor, and the advice she gave which was well beyond her years–advice I took advantage of often.

♥♥♥

Linda was born three weeks premature, weighing 4 pounds, 10 ounces, and only 17 inches long. She was initially hospitalized with pneumonia at 18 months. She suffered from chronic bronchitis.

Born with spinal stenosis and kidney problems, she lived her life in pain, but refused to stay in bed. At 12 years of age, one of the girls in her class bullied her, pushing her from behind, causing Linda to fall flat on her face, breaking her nose in several places. It took three procedures to repair all the damage.

She underwent surgery at 14 to remove multiple breast tumors which ended up being benign. Linda gave herself daily shots of natural growth hormones for four years. She contracted the Epstein-Barr virus at 15, a collagen-vascular disease at 17, and lupus at 19. She had emergency surgery to remove a tumor in her throat when she was 20.

Linda spent a lot of time in hospitals and doctor's offices and at her request, I kept this very private. She wanted no sympathy from others for her physical struggles and never complained when she wasn't feeling well.

While working in a jewelry store on Halloween, Linda was held up at gunpoint. The cold steel barrel pressed firmly against the left temple of a helpless and frightened 21-year-old for an endless, terrifying, horrific, five minutes. The gunman wearing a mask, the stench of his breath all over her face, whispered, "One wrong move and I'll splatter your brains all over this f- - ing counter! The security guard will be back in six minutes, so don't f- - with me."

What the robber didn't know was that Linda had convinced her 72-year-old co-worker to hide in the safe. He wouldn't kill one considering Linda had the keys to all of the display cases, but he would kill two if she faltered which would have drawn his attention to look around the store.

Through all of these adversities, she fought very hard to be an ordinary, active, young adult.

*Linda recuperating after a fever*

One morning, while walking back from one of her many doctor appointments at NYU Medical Center, Linda divulged to me, "Dad, I don't think I am going to live very long. Maybe if I'm lucky I may make 40." (Linda was almost 16 at this time.) "Nonsense, let me inspect your palms," I cajoled, making light of this heart-wrenching revelation. When I looked at Linda's palms, I said, "You are right-handed. Notice this line? This is your lifeline and it is a very long lifeline. Don't worry."

When Linda came down with pneumonia after a prolonged hospital stay a few days before her transition, I remembered our conversation in Manhattan. "She is only 26, not 40. Besides, with constant advancement in medicine, she'll be okay." But things deteriorated.

So when Linda transitioned two days after her 27th birthday, as devastated as I was; not wanting to feel the anguish, the loss, the void, the pain of her death and as much as my selfishness drove me to want her to stay no matter what the cost, I had to accept and recognize this as divine intervention. She had suffered and struggled long enough.

# My Journey

Subsequent to the initial contact the day and night of Linda's transition, I dreamt of her nightly, which was comforting, but was unable in the first few weeks to visit her in an OBE. I was occupied with matters which we all are when the separation and loss occur: the sickness, the suffering, the crying, the loneliness, the grieving process we all endure particularly when it's our child. The wounds from our humanity overshadow the curtain lifting. Our inner judges take over and the guilt begins. We blame ourselves thinking we should have done this or done that or could have done more to prevent it from happening.

As parents, we cannot accept our child is gone. Everything that is right with this world tells us it's not fair. The fear of the finality of suffering and death creates havoc with our minds, hearts, and emotions; our psyches overload. I still cry every day, missing Linda terribly, but she is alive. I know it, having already experienced it. Being human is the most difficult thing asked of us by our higher selves, the guides, messengers, guardian angels, teachers, and healers. The destiny of our souls and our children's souls reveal to us the truth that only a vibration separates the earthly from the heavenly.

But what prepares you for your child's passing? You don't realize it until it is upon you since your whole worldly journey is your training. There is no time or space on the other side; this lifetime and all of your other lifetimes, past, present, and future happen simultaneously, spinning like spokes on a bicycle.

♥♥♥

I can't recall exactly when my training actually began in life, but most probably it was at 13 years of age. My cousin Joseph made his transition in a tragic car accident when he was 20, in April 1970, and nothing was ever the same again. He was in a band and played the drums. We all looked up to him, idolized him, and as young teenagers my cousin John took up drums and I the guitar, and we started our own band.

Joseph was the definition of cool: long hair, extremely good-looking, kind, generous, witty, campy, charismatic, and he lit up the room when he walked in. These were the same adjectives Linda's cousins used to describe her. Joseph was the first person in our family to fulfill his promise to be everyone's teacher before he incarnated in this Earth Life System. At the time we didn't understand the grace he brought to us, the courage he bestowed upon us.

A year later my Aunt Marianne made her transition. She was only 40, but she played the role of aunt, mother, and grandmother to us all because my maternal grandmother, Concetta (Mamie) transitioned when she was only 36, leaving my Uncle Sal, my aunt, and my mother without a mother of their own at ages 12, 7, and 5 respectively. We all prayed to God to spare Aunt Marianne. Her energy was vibrant, her benevolence huge, her generosity enduring. She represented life to us all by giving herself to everyone so selflessly. Why such grief, such misery? I understood back then the separation, the unfolding. I wanted answers, to discover more about the other side.

I distinctly remember my inaugural OBE as an 18-year-old senior at Lafayette High School in Brooklyn. My honors English class professor, Dr. James Fenner, chairman of the department, taught us a meditation technique. I was lying in my bed one night, listening to the stereo with the lights off, going through the meditation steps when I felt a jolt, snapped out of my body, and sat up on my bed. My instinct was to go to the light switch. When I flipped it on, the room remained dark. I turned, saw myself lying in bed and made my way back. I floated into my anatomy, opened my eyes, and the room gradually brightened as if a dimmer were reversed.

In the summer of 1975, while managing a McDonald's on Staten Island, my consciousness was taken over by another person. I was completely relaxed and comforted by this. Then the person spoke, "I am your grandfather, Frank, and I always wanted to meet you. Do you mind if I stay awhile?" I answered, "No, it's my pleasure." My grandfather made his transition six years before I was born. He asked what I was doing and I explained everything to him.

After a couple of minutes he announced, "Thank you so very much for allowing me to be with you," and, as quickly as he came, a messenger from the other side, he left, a vital force channeled in my body.

My mother's best friend Josephine came to visit often. Widowed, with four young children to raise, she possessed the ability to access the other side. Everyone has or had an aunt, grandmother, or mother like Josephine; someone who kept me intrigued with revelations I discern today to be very genuine and real. Back in the late 1970s all of this was still considered paranormal, but to her it was matter-of-fact. Hurray for Josephine!

What followed over the ensuing few years are what I thought to be insignificant happenings. I was able to identify in advance what people wanted to eat, what order songs would be playing on the radio, what streets to drive down to avoid traffic. I knew people's names, ages, birthdays, gender, ages and number of their children, having never met them before. I had several out-of-body encounters on the beach at Fire Island, and I even knew Rodney Dangerfield would show up at a comedy club one night unannounced.

My cousin, an angel named Jessica, came to stay with us for a little more than a year. She made her transfiguration in May 1981. I visited this angel quite often in the hospital, looking into her eyes, holding her, knowing no membrane existed between her and the other side. She dispelled the illusion of death as being so significant, so final. She taught me, as many believe, that when children transition they do not feel the final pain of death, experiencing no discomfort as they shift out of their earthly form; a gift God bestows on his angels who come to teach a lesson, also bequeathing this gift to those of us who emancipate ourselves of our attachments in this domain.

One night in the early 1980s, I watched a program by Shirley MacLaine on OBEs. For those interested in this phenomenon, this woman was probably everyone's teacher. I read her book, *Out on a Limb*, and was wanting more. I picked up a book called *The Llewellyn Practical Guide to Astral Projection*, by Melita Denning and Osborne Phillips, and had some success with their technique.

Then I came across a book called *Journeys Out of the Body*, by Bob Monroe, who turned out to be my guide, my teacher, my messenger in my OBE adventures. Little did I imagine 20 years later, my connection to him and The Monroe Institute®, would be an awakening of consciousness; the final preparation advocating the acceptance of Linda's voyage into the celestial.

Dan Millman was brought to my attention near this same juncture with his books *Way of the Peaceful Warrior* and *No Ordinary Moments*. I paid $50 for a life reading which he sent to me on an audiocassette, transcribing the metaphysical laws that accompanied me in different incarnations, explaining which lives I was presently working through, and revealing to me my ultimate goal of emotional and spiritual freedom on all levels. He showed me the tools I needed, the trials I would face.

When Linda was five years old, I sent him $50 to do a life reading for her and he sent the money back with a note stating he no longer did this type of work, alluding to something I couldn't comprehend at the time, Linda's transition which would precede mine.

A spiritual champion, Ronny, a 17-year-old teenager with a malignant brain tumor, guided me to the Child Life Clinic at Robert Wood Johnson University Hospital in New Brunswick, New Jersey. I went there from 1992 to 1994 not as a dentist, but simply as a volunteer, and spent my time doing what I do best: playing board and video games with the children; reading them books; giving out ice cream, candy, and cookies; making them smile; motivating them; visiting at their beds when they were too sick to get up; and preparing their parents for the journey their children would soon encounter.

Linda and I shared a summer house with several friends in Bradley Beach, New Jersey. She was seven at the time and claimed my friends as her very own with her charming personality, her sense of humor beyond her years. She would have her bathing suit on before 10:00 AM, her pail and shovel ready, and barge into my room. Barely able to contain her excitement, she was on her way to the beach with Millie, Annette, Carmine, or Joe saying, "See you later, alligator," sticking out her tongue and wiggling her fingers behind her ears! Linda was included in all the house barbecues and sleepover parties with *the girls,* and accompanied us to Point Pleasant for a day of rides and fresh sea food. She was the house mascot.

When we returned from the beach every afternoon, Ronny was resting on the porch next door, convalescing, and waiting for Linda. He had a beautiful Dalmatian, Duke. Linda would run up to Duke with all the wonder and innocence

DR. FRANK A. LA BATTO

a young child can possess. Ronny would give Linda treats for Duke and teach her how to make him perform tricks; letting Linda walk Duke around Avon Lake because he was unable to.

Linda was overjoyed due to Ronny's generous nature. He was soft spoken, gentle, courageous, and kind, never bitter or angry, encompassing a big heart, knowing how to make children gleeful, particularly Linda. I am forever grateful, honoring his lovingness towards her. I saw Ronny many times at the Child Life Clinic over the years. When he made his transition, I felt it was necessary to move on.

*Linda, Ronny, and the dogs at Bradley Beach, New Jersey*

I rescued my first soul on 9/11, something I wouldn't be formally trained in until 2004, when I attended the Lifeline® Program at The Monroe Institute (TMI). A woman I had a crush on when we were teenagers made her shift in the World Trade Center disaster.

I went into a meditative state and found her typing at her desk. She saw me, asking, "What are you doing here?" I replied, "There has been an attack and the towers have collapsed. Look around. There are no walls, no people. You are free now. Go to the light. Be happy." I didn't want her to be stuck as so often happens when someone leaves this embodiment suddenly and tragically. She hugged me, turned, and ascended upward.

I was given the gift of holding a grandchild in October 2006. My cousin Robert and his wife Natalie had their first child, Justin, and I went to pay them a visit. While I was holding Justin, my godmother Marion, who transitioned a year earlier, made me an offer I couldn't refuse! She asked to occupy my body to hold her grandson.

It is rapturous to appreciate what a grandparent savors when they hold their grandchild for the first time. It is different from holding your own child, as those with grandchildren can attest to; the pride, the gratification, the tenderness, a miracle in all its splendor. I cried tears of rejoicing, my aunt's amongst my own. It was breathtaking. Aunt Marion, another heavenly liaison, permitting me to hold her grandchild, was preparing me for what lay ahead.

♥♥♥

When parents pass first they become our messengers. It is their purpose for our existence, the so-called natural order of things. My mother, Evangeline, transitioned in June 1979, at the age of 47, leaving my youngest sister Marianne without a mother at seven, repeating a pattern in our family that occurred generation upon generation.

I had dreams of my mother as we all do when a parent is gone, but made no contact in an OBE until my father left in February 2002. The day of my father's departure, my cordless kitchen phone stopped working. A week later, out of frustration, I threw the phone against the wall and the batteries came flying out. Several days went by and I finally picked the phone off the floor, replaced the batteries, and put the phone back in its cradle. It still refused to work.

One evening a month afterward, an OBE ensued . . . WALKING MY FATHER UP THE STEPS TO HIS BEDROOM, MY MOTHER APPEARS AT THE DOORWAY. HE LAMENTS, "VAN, I DID ALL I COULD, I FAILED." SHE HOLDS OUT HER ARMS REPLYING, "NICK, COME WITH ME. EVERYTHING WILL BE OKAY." THEY BOTH WALK INTO THE BEDROOM AND MOVE UP INTO THE INFINITE . . .

The following morning, the phone began to work and did so for eight more years. My father was communicating to me he wasn't ready to leave this realm until my mother came for him that night.

My father inhabited my body three times subsequent to his passing in order to make actual contact with his best friend, my godfather, Uncle Lou. Each time my father entered my body, Uncle Lou knew it was my father who was shaking his hand and hugging him, not me. "I smell his cologne. I recognize his touch," Uncle Lou would say at each occurrence.

Patients would appear facing me at night at the foot of my bed asking me to contact their families to tell them that they are alive on the other side. I even found the son of one of my patients who died tragically at 19 years of age. He loves his father so much and wanted him to know he is at peace and it wasn't his father's fault he left so suddenly. My patient received a huge healing and cried in my arms.

Relatives and friends who have crossed over constantly contact me because they know I have learned how to communicate with them. I accept it as real, normal, something we are all capable of. *Your mind is like a parachute. It works best when it's open.*

♥♥♥

My time together with Linda was amazing, magical, special, one-on-one. I was fortunate and blessed; admiring her courage, determination, vigor, and fight to constantly want to do as many activities as possible while battling physical afflictions and surgeries, enduring endless hours in doctor's offices and hospitals.

She filled my essence with beautiful memories: me doing impersonations of her favorite childhood characters, playing board games, occupying hours on end with Sesame Street Village and Mickey Mouse Roller Coaster, watching movies, going on vacations, swimming in our pool, burying me in the sand at the beach, horseback riding, pitching baseball in the yard, basketball in the playroom, shopping for all her clothes in the mall, breakfasts at the diner, cooking her favorite meals of chicken cutlets and raviolis, dinners at fancy restaurants, late night trips to Carvel gazing at the universe in wonderment while we enjoyed our ice cream.

We sledded down the hill behind our house, built snowmen, ice skated, biked, sang songs, danced, and roller bladed together.

I entertained her friends with countless sleepovers, put her braces on, took her back and forth to college, moved her in and out of dorm rooms and her apartments, and bought her first car. I was school parent for every excursion and event, sneaking into the schoolyard and playing with her and her friends during lunchbreak; coaching her middle school softball team.

I remember feeling how lucky I was to chaperone her 8th grade prom, witnessing her radiance when she was asked to dance by a boy who had a crush on her (even with her braces and broken nose). My eyes welled up with tears.

I meditated for hours by the river in Red Bank, New Jersey, while she took singing and acting lessons, feeling the exhilaration of our lives together as the current ebbed majestically below my feet. I videotaped countless hours of Linda since her birth to her mid-20s and took over four thousand photographs.

If the story ends here, I can declare Linda is very much alive in my films and photos. However, just as demonstrable as this documentation is of physical certainty, I will present as convincingly and verifiably, documentation of Linda in the non-physical and proof that there is no death, just a continuation, a flow, a shift from one embodiment to the next.

# June 2012

Linda's journey on the other side and my journey on this side began to intersect. I can recall with the utmost clarity what it felt like to return to my office those first few weeks -- I simply did not want to be there! I had just lost my daughter and wanted to stay in bed and cry all day. And boy, did I cry!

But Linda, familiar with my specialized dental practice because she worked alongside me many a summer and in-between her career choices, forced me out of the house.

I began to treat children with facial deformities after my two-year plastic surgery residency.

I also treat patients who suffer from extreme fear and anxiety wounded by circumstances from this and other lifetimes. They rely on my advanced training in Pediatrics, Orthodontics, Endodontics, Prosthetics, Cosmetics, Implants, and Periodontics to help them. I maintain a General Practice utilizing sedation and have a dental lab on the premises allowing me to move swiftly, smoothly, and simultaneously between specialties.

Every morning Linda interjected in my ear, "Dad, take me to the office with you. I'll help you with your patients." I would get in my car, dejected. Linda would be sitting adjoining me as she did so often during our physical life together. "Remember when we drove to the Jersey Shore we would sing 'A Whole New World' from *Aladdin*, or songs from *Beauty and the Beast*. Let's do that while we drive together."

Each day she would recommend a different song. I began to look forward to my enchanted drives with her. At the office, she constantly reminded me of her presence, moving papers, flickering lights, appearing to Jenna, one of my gifted employees, who would notice Linda sitting at my desk as a young girl.

♥♥♥

I knew intuitively from my guidance there was healing work to be done, to assist Linda in her ascension in the light. I called my very dear friend Karen Malik, Senior Facilitator at TMI for 36 years, developer of the Gateway Voyage® and Exploration Essence Programs, long time student of A.H. Almaas and his spiritual teaching The Diamond Approach, expressing my concerns. She invited me to attend a Lifeline Program the week of June 16th.

As our phone conversation ended, I received a call from Jeannie Callahan, a close friend of my wife, Susan. Jeannie, a massage therapist, said she felt I could use a massage and wanted to provide her services to me at no charge.

Little did I fathom when I arrived at her massage quarters at Sky Athletic Club in Rockville Centre, New York, on June 6th, I would find an accomplished medium, channeler, healer, Reiki Master, and author of the book "Disguised Blessings." This would be the beginning of a two-year relationship guided by Linda from the other side. I have since sent many, many friends, family members, and patients to Jeannie who have benefited from her talents and capabilities.

"We have a visitor," Jeannie articulated as the session unfolded. Immediately through my Reiki training I felt vibrations. Linda began to enunciate, "I wanted to express my love to you in so many different ways while on Earth, but, given the ego and the human condition, I was blocked from expressing true essential, unlimited perfection." I asked Linda if I could help her on this side and on the other side. Linda enabled Jeannie to feel enormous reverence, great respect, and admiration for me; her devotion so overwhelming that Jeannie started to weep, stopping the massage. I interjected, "What can I do for you?" Linda responded, "Write the book."

Linda continued, but began speaking in the present, [a phenomenon that will occur throughout this book because of no time on the other side]. "I am sent here to be your teacher, to teach you humility. I respect and admire the work you do on yourself in this lifetime." I verbalize, "I am honored to be your father. I want to work with you on both sides so you can ascend in the light."

At this moment in the session Jeannie channels Linda as a little girl in her bedroom in my house in Old Bridge. She is very jubilant. Entities often appear to mediums as young children, a time in their lives when they are most lighthearted, living in a pure, innocent, consummate, loving state. Linda proudly points to all her trophies for baseball and karate. Jeannie sees Linda taking a bath and smells Linda's bedroom as Linda tells her, "clean and fresh."

. . . I SHIFT INTO AN OBE. I FINISH RUNNING FIVE-YEAR-OLD LINDA'S BUBBLE BATH, SETTING OUT JOHNSON'S BABY SHAMPOO TO WASH HER HAIR. "DAD," SHE CALLS FROM THE BATHROOM, "WHEN I'M COVERED WITH BUBBLES YOU CAN COME IN. I SHALL BE ARIEL AND YOU SEBASTIAN. URSULA IS PLOTTING SOMETHING EVIL. WE HAVE TO WARN KING TRITON BEFORE IT'S TOO LATE!"

I OPEN THE BATHROOM DOOR AND FIND LINDA SWIMMING LAZILY IN THE TUB; HER HAIR, ARMS, LEGS, AND TORSO COVERED IN BUBBLES. I CAN ONLY GLIMPSE HER ROUND, GLITTERING FACE, FILLED WITH UNCONTROLLABLE ENTHUSIASM. SHE EXCLAIMS WITH ANTICIPATION IN

HER VOICE, MIMICKING ARIEL, GIGGLING, "SEBASTIAN. QUICK. HURRY!" TEARY-EYED, I PUT ON MY JAMAICAN ACCENT, "WHAT IS IT MY LITTLE ONE? WHO IS IN DANGER?" . . .

Jeannie now enlightens me, "Your adoration concerning Linda is helping her reach a summit. Linda needs to rest now. She is with Mother Mary and the angels. The transitional shift from the embodiment is very trying for the individual."

At the end of the massage, Jeannie continues, "Linda is still here. She wants you to return and is calling me, 'honey.'" (Linda uses that word to describe people she admires and befriends.) Jeannie asks my permission to take Linda to a prayer group this evening. I agree as long as Linda isn't near negative entities. Upon leaving, Jeannie informs me she went down to the beach this morning to meditate, asking Linda to use her body as an instrument to aide in communicating with me.

At our second session on June 13th, Linda is in the suite. She is herself as a little girl playing hide-and-go-seek. Linda expresses to Jeannie she cherishes yellow flowers and wants me to have them in my chambers while she is with me during the Lifeline Program next week. Linda shows Jeannie a yellow rosebush at our house on Long Island, explaining to us she is the one who tells my cousin Patricia to buy it. (I verified this purchase with my cousin asking why she bought a yellow rosebush. Patricia replied, "I was in the nursery and couldn't decide to buy a red or yellow one. Then a voice in my head said, 'Buy the yellow one.'")

Linda reveals, "Dad, it is important to do the work on your side before the voyage to our side. People think once they leave their bodies, they go to heaven. They must attain higher levels by working on their egos during their physical life –petty hatreds, animosities, and jealousies. Pure unconditional love is what we come into this life to learn. I am learning these lessons on my side (other side) working with angels, guides, and healers. Pray to me and others who transition to help us in our work to attain the ultimate resonance.

"Many are aware they need to do work in their lives but are blocked via physical illnesses and injuries. Sometimes the blockage is so overbearing a soul can choose to transcend earlier to do their spiritual work in the infinite. If you have help on both sides you can more easily complete your process and never have to return for more earthly lifetimes. Everyone eventually attains paradise because God is all good and loving."

I answer, "I shall help you next week so you can rise up to a higher vibration." Linda is letting Jeannie experience overwhelming homage for me. Jeannie states Linda is being held and helped not only by Mother Mary, but my sister Terry as well (who made her transition in July 2011 at the young age of 51).

♥♥♥

As evolving beings, we are here to develop a higher mind and soul. We all have our frailties. The basic survival instincts, forged into our DNA thousands of years ago, still remain with us today. These antiquated qualities of our lower selves are why we are incarnated. Once we have worked through these lesser frequencies, we liberate ourselves and our loved ones who crossover before us and we end our Earth Life Cycles, unencumbered to move to non-physical absoluteness forever immortal.

We all have different abilities in learning how to communicate with those who have moved on; whether by touch, sound, sight, smell, music, meditation, or OBE, to name just a few.

I share Linda's and my journey, our path, our knowing, one that is familiar to many. Keep in mind, ours is only one of an infinite number of ways of connecting with loved ones and all are valid, real, and affirming. Our higher selves choose a journey that is right for our individual growth and development. In spirituality, simple is best and "all roads lead to Rome."

♥♥♥

On Saturday, June 16th, I arrive at TMI to attend a week-long Lifeline Program being held at Roberts Mountain Retreat house, the home of Bob Monroe during his earthly life, at the foot of the Blue Ridge Mountains in Faber, Virginia. It is a magical place. Bob is truly in attendance always making himself known to me.

Lifeline teaches and trains you how to make contact with souls who have transitioned to the non-physical. This program is extremely valuable because it confirms without a doubt the reality of life beyond physical existence. Having already experienced a Lifeline Program in June 2004, I am immediately able to contact, communicate, and interact with Linda, and she with me, as soon as I set foot at TMI.

Karen Malik lines the hallway leading to my quarters with yellow flowers and has a beautiful country grown yellow floral bouquet on my bureau. Feeling Linda's presence, I immediately set photos of her on the dresser. Throughout the week participants, staff members, and Karen, enter my room to marvel at the substantive vivacity of Linda.

Each morning, walking barefoot on dew-laden fields, Linda enters my body asking, "Allow me to smell the aroma of fresh-cut grass, to feel its coolness beneath your feet. It reminds me so much of our days at the beach when we used to hold hands, the water brushing against us."

We end up at the tree-lined edge along the mountainside; the preliminary rays of the sun shining through the leaves, the early morning air, cool and refreshing, the song of birds and God's creatures moving about the underbrush. Here in the glory of creation no barriers exist between this world and the hereafter, just the beauty of everlasting life. Linda and I are twin souls vibrating as one being.

My lunchtime promenades with Linda take us down winding roads. She points out singular yellow wildflowers among the white and lavender ones, whispering in my ear, "I will always be with you."

My first Father's Day without Linda falls during my week in Virginia. I brought a card from home Linda had given me some years back and read it that Sunday morning:

**A Father's Day Prayer**
**For You, Father**

May God be ever at your side
And grant that every day
Will bring its gift
Of pleasant hours
And sunny skies your way–
God give you the strength
For all your needs
And rest and comfort, too–
God bless you with His perfect love
And grant good health to you.

**Happy Father's Day**
**I Love You**
**Linda**

. . . WHILE SITTING AT MY DESK FINISHING THE POEM, I FIND MYSELF IN AN OBE BEING WHISKED BACK IN TIME. LINDA PERMEATES MY BODY. SHE IS ONLY THREE YEARS OLD. WE

ARE AT CLOVE LAKE PARK ON STATEN ISLAND, PRETENDING WE ARE IN THE HUNDRED ACRE WOOD WITH WINNIE THE POOH, SKIPPING STONES ALONG THE FLOWING STREAM, CLIMBING ROCKS, SEARCHING FOR HONEY WITH CHRISTOPHER ROBIN. "DAD, WE MUST CROSS THE STREAM TO GET TIGGER TO HELP US. WINNIE IS STUCK IN THE TREE. HE CAN'T GET OUT."

SHE RELEASES MY HAND, RUNNING AHEAD TO THE FOOTBRIDGE WAVING HER ARMS. "COME ON DAD. COME ON CHRISTOPHER ROBIN." I AM OVERCOME WITH PURE EXULTATION. SHE IS EXISTING INSIDE OF ME. WE ARE ONE; MY HEART CELEBRATING, YET BROKEN. MY HEALING INITIATES AND THE VEIL LIFTS . . .

During the Lifeline sessions, Bob Monroe, who made his transition on March 17th, 1995, guides you to various focus levels which facilitate altered states of consciousness. Bob describes these focus levels (states) you travel through using Hemi-Sync®, a sound pattern technology that synchronizes brain waves in each hemisphere, simply numbering them from 1 through 49. But I find it is Karen's voice doing the guiding at key points when contact with Linda is made.

Monday morning in Focus 12, the State of Expanded Awareness, I have an OBE . . . THE SNOW IS COMING DOWN VERY HARD ON THIS FEBRUARY AFTERNOON. TEN-YEAR-OLD LINDA AND I ARE IN MY DEN IN OLD BRIDGE. SHE IS IN A RED AND GREEN STRIPED SWEATER, JEANS, AND WHITE SOCKS. I SMELL THE CORNISH HENS AND SWEET POTATOES IN THE OVEN. SHE PICKS UP THE MICROPHONE, DANCING SIDE TO SIDE, MOVING, SWAYING, SINGING "THE MAIN EVENT" ALONG WITH BARBRA STREISAND, TRYING TO HIT THE HIGH NOTES.

WHEN SHE CONCLUDES SINGING SHE TAKES A BOW. I APPLAUD AND SHE LAUGHS, "MAKE BELIEVE WE'RE STUCK ON AN ISLAND NOW AND WE NEED THE COUCH TO BE A RAFT SO WE

CAN FLOAT AWAY." AS I JUMP ABOARD SHE CONTINUES, "WE CAN USE THE PILLOWS AND THE BLANKETS TO KEEP US WARM AND COMFORTABLE AT NIGHT."

I ENTER FOCUS 21, THE STATE BETWEEN PHYSICAL AND NON-PHYSICAL REALITY, LINDA IS PRESENT AS A 19-YEAR-OLD AND WE DANCE TO "THE BEST THINGS HAPPEN WHILE YOU'RE DANCING" FROM *WHITE CHRISTMAS*. STILL IN AN OUT-OF-BODY STATE, I AM ACTUALLY HOLDING HER, PICKING HER UP, TWIRLING AND DIPPING HER. I LOOK AT HER FACE, BEHOLDING HER INTENT ON GETTING THE STEPS RIGHT. THE FIREPLACE IS GIVING OFF WARMTH ON A COLD DECEMBER NIGHT. WE ARE BOTH SMILING, PEERING INTO EACH OTHER'S EYES, KNOWING NO MOMENT EXCEPT THIS. LAUGHING, DANCING, SPINNING—SHE IS INDISPUTABLY ALIVE.

CONTINUING THIS OBE, WE ARRIVE AT FOCUS 27, THE RECEPTION CENTER, WHERE WE ARE MET BY LOVED ONES AND GUIDES, AND CREATE A SPECIAL PLACE TO REST. THERE WE GO TO A BEACH HOUSE, OUR SPECIAL PLACE, WHERE LINDA, AS HER ADULT SELF, BRINGS HORSES FOR US TO RIDE; MINE, A PALOMINO, HERS, A CHESTNUT BROWN THOROUGHBRED MARE WITH A WHITE DIAMOND PATCH ON ITS FOREHEAD. WE GALLOP ALONG THE WATER'S EDGE, THE HORSES SWEATING FROM THE SUN. I AM BOUNCING UP AND DOWN IN THE SADDLE, MY BUTT HURTING. LINDA, FAR IN FRONT OF ME, STOPS, DISMOUNTS, AND DIVES INTO THE OCEAN FOR A SWIM. "TONIGHT," SHE SUGGESTS, "WE'LL THROW A PARTY!" . . .

♥♥♥

. . . I RETURN THAT EVENING IN AN OBE TO FOCUS 27 AND AM TAKEN TO A BEAUTIFUL ITALIAN VILLA ON A HILLSIDE, WITH A VINEYARD AND A WATERFALL. (IN THIS FOCUS LEVEL, WE CAN ALL CREATE A DWELLING IN THE UNEMBODIED WHERE WE REST AND REJUVENATE, COMPLETE WITH EVERYTHING WE NEED TO BRING HAPPINESS AND PEACE TO OUR ELEVATED SELVES BEYOND OUR EARTHLY LIVES.) LINDA HAS PARTY GLOBES STRUNG ALONG THE VILLA MATCHING A 1940s MOVIE SET, AN ERA SHE GREATLY REVELS IN. VINTAGE CARS PULL UP.

RELATIVES AND FRIENDS WHO HAVE TRANSITIONED ARE ESCORTED TO AN OUTDOOR DINNER PARTY; EATING, DRINKING WINE, AND DANCING TO SWING MUSIC.

LINDA AND I DESCEND TO THE WATER'S EDGE, LISTENING TO THE WAVES CRASH, HEARING SONG AND LAUGHTER IN THE BACKGROUND. DOLPHINS JUMP OUT OF THE OCEAN WHILE DOGS AND CATS ROAM FREELY IN THE SAND. I AM HAVING A FANTASTIC ADVENTURE, NOT WANTING TO LEAVE. LINDA GRABS MY HAND GESTURING, "I AM VERY ELATED HERE BUT THERE IS WORK WE MUST DO." I REPLY, "THIS IS WHY WE ARE HERE THIS WEEK, BUSINESS AND PERSONAL. DON'T TELL DON CORLEONE." WE BOTH BREAK OUT INTO UNCONTROLLABLE HILARITY. LINDA FALLS IN THE SAND, HYSTERICALLY SHOUTING OUT, "I'M GOING TO HAVE TO TINKLE, I CAN'T STOP LAUGHING." "CAN YOU TINKLE IN THE NON-PHYSICAL?" I ASK. WE ROAR EVEN HARDER! . . .

♥♥♥

On Tuesday evening I relive Linda's transition. Witnessing your child's death is the most painful thing for a parent to do and requires enormous courage to endure.

. . . I ENTER AN OBE STATE AND GO TO FOCUS 27. I MEET LINDA AT THE BEACH HOUSE, INSTRUCTING OUR HIGHER SELVES TO GO BACK TO HER PHYSICAL FORM ON MAY 7TH. HOVERING OVER LINDA I SAY, "YOU WILL SOON MAKE YOUR TRANSITION AND BE FREE. I AM WITH YOU WHEN YOU ENTER THIS MATERIAL FORM AND AM HONORED TO BE WITH YOU WHEN YOU LEAVE IT."

WITH THAT, LINDA EXPERIENCES A JOLT AND HER SOUL SEPARATES AND RISES. SEEING THERE IS NO TIME OR SPACE ON THE OTHER SIDE, I AM ACTUALLY WITH HER DURING HER FINAL EARTHLY MOMENT . . .

The comforting fact is no one embarks upon this voyage alone. You are surrounded by loved ones and yourselves from other incarnations who have already made this transition.

♥♥♥

There is a focus level where people can sometimes remain stuck because they have not yet let go of their attachments to physical reality; still believing they are earthbound. Bob Monroe named this level Focus 23, the State where Souls Go when They Transition. It is here where work must be done to help people to recognize they have indeed crossed over and are now free to ascend to the lofty vibrations of Focus 27.

. . . ON WEDNESDAY, AS I ENTER AN OBE AT FOCUS 23, LINDA WANTS TO GO BACK TO HER TWO YORKSHIRE TERRIERS AND HER FOUR CATS. RETURNING TO HER APARTMENT, THE ANIMALS, SENSING HER TANGIBILITY, BARK AND MEOW AS LINDA HUGS THEM ALL. KNOWING ANIMALS HAVE A CONSCIOUSNESS AND WILL JOIN US, LINDA REALIZES IT ISN'T NECESSARY TO REMAIN IN A DIMINISHED VIBRATION. SHE CAN ASCEND INTO THE CLARITY OF FOCUS 27 CONSIDERING SHE IS RELEASING WORLDLY ATTACHMENTS, WHICH WILL LEAD TO BREAKING THE CYCLE OF INCARNATIONS.

LINDA NOW ASKS TO ACCOMPANY ME TO PERFORM SOUL RETRIEVALS. LINDA AND I TRAVEL FROM FOCUS 27 TO FOCUS 23 FREEING THOSE STUCK IN THE NOISE OF TEMPORAL CONSCIOUSNESS BECAUSE THEY ARE UNAWARE THEY HAVE ALREADY MADE THEIR TRANSITION. THE ELEVATED SOULS WHOM WE BRING TO FOCUS 27 RECOGNIZE THEY HAVE EXITED OUT OF THEIR CARNAL BODIES. ALONGSIDE MY SISTER TERRY AND WITH MY EXPERTISE IN RETRIEVALS, WE RESCUE MANY, MANY SOULS, MOSTLY CHILDREN, BRINGING THEM INTO THE EVERLASTING . . .

It is a glorious week of unlimited fulfillment, brilliance, and enchanting places surpassing imagination. For me, I am living on the other side without having a near-death experience (NDE).

*Linda and her Aunt Terry*

I undergo an NDE and am totally vital and healthy. It happened on Thursday, October 23rd, 2008, during a session in the Starlines II Program developed by Dr. Franceen King, a facilitator at TMI, who also developed the Exploration 27® and Starlines Program. I move into Focus 49, the Star Gate. There I am unequivocally free, far beyond any previous OBE. I am alive, bathing in the bliss of limitless, unmitigated, absolute completion, understanding all knowing, viewing colors, and encountering beauty incomprehensible in physical reality. It is home, more real than any breath I have ever taken; just as anyone who has had an NDE has ever come back to report. Ironically, thinking of leaving Linda is the driving force that eventually leads me back into this world.

Two books I read subsequent to Linda's passing explain in great detail this event; one is *To Heaven and Back,* by Dr. Mary C. Neal and the other is *Heaven is for Real,* by Todd Burpo. I deeply honor and respect those who have been chosen by God to have an NDE; miraculously returning to the terrestrial, battling unimaginable somatic struggles in order to help us to envision the intangible as undeniable.

♥♥♥

On Friday morning my week at Lifeline concludes. After our morning walk together, I place Linda's photos back in my suitcase and have breakfast. When I return to my room, Linda's sparkle is gone. Everything is quiet and still, but once again guidance is telling me more work needs to be done.

As I am leaving TMI, Karen says to me, "Your work with Linda is miraculous, but there are more miracles ahead. Linda will reveal herself on a regular basis with conclusive, factual, pertinent information of the eternal–her gift to you. Continue your sessions with Jeannie, bringing third-party verification of the truth already sustained in the Lifeline Program. This confirmation is very important to those who are searching for ways to lift the covering of grief in order to accept the genuine revelation of the other side as natural and readily accessible."

# The Difficult Journey

**W**hat I am about to disclose are encounters that break my heart, experienced by Linda during her time on Earth, adding to her struggles, but need to be cleared in order for her to make her final ascension in the light. These revelations are extremely painful for me to bear witness to. (The other side is timeless. All conversations and interactions with Linda are always in the now, in the present, a way of communication different than we are used to.)

♥♥♥

On June 24th, in a session with Jeannie, Linda takes us back to her wake and funeral, an event that she and every soul that passes is present for; listening and feeling to what everyone is doing and saying. Linda shows Jeannie that I am pacing back and forth, permitting Jeannie and me to partake in the grief, sadness, and distress of all who arrive to pay their respects, a very moving occurrence.

Linda acknowledges, "There is one person in particular who opens her heart to me, a diabetic, and will undergo some heart problems. I shall help that person." (One family member becomes very ill shortly after the funeral.)

Jeannie tells me major healers are in the room standing next to Linda. They are performing healing over my Heart and Third Eye Chakras (Chakras are main energy centers and wheel-like spinning vortexes connected to major organs). These healers will be working on me for three days, mostly at night while I sleep, preparing me for what lies ahead. I am to drink plenty of water and get a lot of rest. [I remember quite vividly looking into Linda's eyes at night during this period.]

In a session on July 1st, Linda takes me to the other side. She allows Jeannie to hear the sounds of twigs breaking and leaves rustling, showing Jeannie us hiking up the mountain behind the cabin at TMI where Linda guides my steps so I don't slip and sprain my ankle.

Then, the following truths are spoken by Linda: "There are escalating planes a soul moves through as it works in the heavens. You can access parallel lives by reliving them or parts of them in order to accomplishing healing." She then asks me to re-enact hardships that wounded her during her lifetimes inhibiting her growth. She wants to relive these lessons, gain the knowledge, and resolve them so she can eventually be free from the Earth Life System.

Linda is aware of my training and expeditions in Timeline, a program developed by Lee Stone, also a facilitator at TMI. One of the many things you learn in this program is how to go back in physical time, relive your youth, and assist your younger self using your present-day knowledge and wisdom.

Doing this allows you to free yourself of patterns carried over from other lifetimes; excelling your learning curve in the Earth Life System eventually freeing yourself from physical manifestations. An excellent book on this subject is *Many Lives, Many Masters*, by Dr. Brian Weiss.

You also learn how to interact with your higher self in the non-physical state, the state beyond time (no-time) as we know it, and help and guide others who have transitioned work with their higher selves to complete their journey in the light.

♥♥♥

I tell Jeannie my higher self is standing alongside Linda's higher self. Linda takes me back to when she is 11 years old in middle school being bullied by a group of girls who inflict a lot of emotional misery. I stand behind Linda, putting my hands on her pre-teen shoulders. Linda shouts, "Enough pushing me around. I am loved by my parents and I have self-worth. I am very secure, athletic, smart, and well-liked and I refuse to have you bring me down with your jealousies and insecurities. You are abused bodily, psychologically, emotionally, and mentally by your parents and so-called friends, and I am not."

Linda then releases pain, dejection, and abuse, showing Jeannie these girls as adults, still at it, reigning degradation on their children, spouses, and friends. Linda is allowing us to process this with her.

Linda becomes more empowered and vibrates at an elevated frequency. We go to the home of one of Linda's high school teachers. This woman manipulates, exploits, and berates Linda, preying upon her substantiated illnesses and wounds caused via the bullying.

Pretending to be her friend, this teacher uses her control and influence over Linda, assailing her, inflicting emotional and psychological abuse. She derives sadistic pleasure in exerting her power over Linda.

As I stand next to Linda's higher self with my higher self, my arms on Linda's teenage shoulders, we are enveloped in a golden encasement of grace. This teacher remains in total darkness. Linda shakes her fists yelling out, "No more, no more, never again." I say to Linda, "It is okay, we can leave now." But Linda endures, manifesting as a young woman, "No more shall I ever permit the darkness and evil which you and others like you possess from encompassing my being!"

Linda allows Jeannie to tolerate how sick this person is. Jeannie feels nauseous, dizzy, sits down, stops channeling and shockingly declares, "I have never channeled an entity this dark, demented, and heinous before. Linda is revealing there is one to come who is far worse!" Jeannie has to rid the negative consumption of this being in order to initiate unbounded healing.

Linda has me accompany her to a male figure she is dating. Waving her hands, Linda expounds, "No more, no more, never again!" She shows us his nefarious spiral of toxicity.

As Linda turns away from him she decrees, "I am clear of all this vehemence now. I love you so much Dad." Jeannie and I embrace Linda's overwhelming gratitude to us considering the work we have accomplished.

Then Linda resumes, "Do you have the strength and courage to move ahead? I want to be released from earthly embodiments and only bring unrestricted elation in the light." We enter an amphitheater filled with relatives and friends and Linda is indicating to them how hurt, angry, and disappointed she is. Their names are revealed to me. They speak behind her back, casting judgments: she clears this indignation and expands further. At this point she reveals to me and Jeannie the most painful of truths.

Linda takes Jeannie and me to a physician's office showing us a malicious, evil, hideous, warped individual. Prior to setting foot in his office, anointed guides, guardian angels, the Holy Spirit, and Mother Mary surround us; enveloping a powerful white shroud of all-encompassing immaculate protection around us and also placing an encasement over the doctor so his ferocity can no longer harm others.

"Dad," Linda pronounces, "He's prescribing the wrong medications to me on purpose, doing it to all his young patients, never conferring with any primary care providers. He misdiagnoses to manipulate and keep us coming back to him causing our illnesses to progress. You never treat any of your patients this way. Look in the box you took from my apartment and there you will find the medications he gives me which cause my condition to deteriorate."

Jeannie is able to contact the pure evil and darkness in his soul and says, "The angels, healers, and masters are showing me he exists in the dark side; well entrenched in the medical community, deeply rooted politically through money, exerting satanic influence over them. They are showing me a courtroom not of bodily substance, where he will be tried and sentenced for the souls he willingly and knowingly destroyed on this planet."

Linda proclaims to me, "I am finally clear of all judgments, negativity, darkness, and the patterns connected with them. I have completed the unresolved lessons of all lives and have finished my cycles in the Earth Life System. It is no longer necessary for me to incarnate, and, if you continue your work, you will be emancipated too. We spent many, many lifetimes together and I am honored and humble for your help on both sides."

Linda makes her Earth-life episodes into a speck and they dissolve. She is such an advanced soul, becoming physical is no longer required. She is now the teacher. Commending Linda I announce, "I am grateful given the strength, courage, guidance, training, and wisdom you bestow, allowing me to assist you on your journey." Jeannie and I hear songs of praise by Linda and the angels, seeing them bowing to us in homage.

Linda takes us to a place of magnificent colors, beauty, and oscillations. She discloses to Jeannie the names of those friends and relatives who show her dedication, reverence, kindness, and compassion during her earthly sojourn. Linda confers upon them endless appreciation and indebtedness. She gives blessings on those doctors and physical therapists who were kind to her, helping her from their hearts, healers devoted to their mission and calling. Linda's voice is much clearer. She ascends to the highest level in the light.

. . . I AM PULLED INTO AN OBE AT THE END OF THIS SESSION. IT IS A DAMP, WINDY DAY; A DRIZZLE DESCENDING UPON MY FACE AS I WAIT OUTSIDE. THE LIMOUSINE THAT WILL TAKE LINDA AND HER FRIENDS TO THE PROM HAS PULLED INTO THE DRIVEWAY. LINDA STANDS IN THE THRESHOLD WEARING A SLEEVELESS PINK FLOWERY GOWN, DONNING A PINK SHAWL, A PEARL WHITE NECKLACE WITH MATCHING DANGLING PEARL EARRINGS, A WHITE POCKETBOOK AND WHITE CARNATIONS ON HER WRIST. HER FACE IS BEAMING. "IS THIS WHAT SHE WILL LOOK LIKE WHEN SHE GETS MARRIED?" I WHISPER. IT IS A MOMENT OF FASCINATION AND HAPPINESS; A FUTURE OF UNQUESTIONABLE JOY.

LINDA DESCENDS THE STEPS AS I HOLD HER WAIST AND SMELL THE SCENT OF GROWN-UP PERFUME, HER HAIRSPRAY KEEPING HER LONG, WAVY HAIR FROM BEING DISTURBED BY THE WEATHER. I CAN'T TELL IF SHE IS TREMBLING FROM THE EXCITEMENT OR THE COLD OR BOTH. "YOU LOOK BEAUTIFUL," I INFORM HER WHILE GIVING HER A SOFT KISS ON HER RIGHT CHEEK NOT TO SPOIL HER MAKEUP. SHE ASKS, "DID I DO A GOOD JOB THE WAY YOU TAUGHT ME WHEN I WAS A KID?" WE BOTH HAVE A BETWEEN-US LAUGH. IT WAS ALL WORTH IT CONSIDERING THIS MOMENT. TEARS OF PRIDE WELL UP IN MY EYES . . .

*Linda in prom dress*

DR. FRANK A. LA BATTO

That afternoon, while in the hot tub, Linda inhabits my body and we experience relaxation and happiness as the jets massage us. I am encompassed in complete, unending, elation; bathing in ecstasy, feeling frivolous and gay, overcome with peace, exhilaration, and appreciation of our accomplishments only a few hours before.

Then she moves out, rests alongside me and makes small talk, asking me about work, the house, Susan, and plans for the upcoming weekend. It is so incontestable, so consummate. She bequeaths, "I give you this gift of us together for you allow it to happen. A soul, once free, can divide itself into infinite particles being everywhere spontaneously and simultaneously. This is the miracle of creation, the limitless possibilities of heaven." I hear parts of the James Taylor song, "Something in the Way She Moves," as I tilt my head back:

Well there's something in the way she moves

Looks my way, or calls my name

That seems to leave this troubled world behind

And if I'm feeling down and blue

Or troubled by some foolish game

She always seem to make me change my mind –

Every now and then the things I lean on lose their meaning

And I find myself careening

In the places where I should not let me go

She has the power to go where no one else can find me

Yes, and silently remind me

Of the happiness and good times that I know –

It isn't what she's got to say

Or how she thinks or where she's been

To me, the words are nice, the way they sound
I like to hear them best that way
She says them mostly just to calm me down - -
And I feel fine anytime she's around me now
She's around me now
I guess just about all of the time and
If I'm well you can tell, she's been with me now
She's been with me now
Quite a long, long time
Yes, and I feel fine

♥♥♥

Linda allows us to experience with her in the non-physical the rescuing of parts of herself in the Earth Life Cycle just completed, which is in actuality the incarnation of past and future lives she still needs to work through. Rescuing these parts negates the necessity of re-entering human physicality to gain wisdom in order to move on.

When I and others do soul retrievals, we retrieve a soul from the currently completed Earth Life Cycle, so the soul can work with guides, teachers, and healers on the other side and decide if it is necessary to endure additional lifetimes. But I believe this is the first time I or anyone else has witnessed while still on Earth a soul's final ascension in the light, something we will all celebrate on the other side.

# In the Light

Linda now resides fully in the highest vibration in the light, free to create, heal, guide, and motivate, as you will soon discover.

I meet Jeannie on July 6th, and I am able to reach a young Linda immediately. She shows me a beautiful waterfall embedded in a mountainside with lush, green vegetation; a deep, blue ocean of vibrant, transparent colors; a pure lavender sky with soft orange, yellow, and white billowy clouds in the distance and birds singing in harmony, reminding me of the peaceful tranquility of Maui. She jumps from a tree into a river below while other children are shouting and swinging from swings made of rope hanging lazily on the branches.

"Is this what the other side is like?" I ask as Jeannie and I perceive the fragrance of the cooling afternoon summer breeze. Linda replies, "The best way to explain it is to imagine a holographic three-dimensional perfect reality. All sounds, scents of flowers, landscapes, skies, and waters are surrounded by a benevolent, bountiful grace. We breathe in a vibrational 360° motion, not in and out as on Earth. All beings are separate, yet one. By creating on the other side we contribute to the adventures on your side (Earth). I shall send you a sign so you will be able to understand."

♥♥♥

A small miracle occurs on Sunday, August 19th. A rosebush, dormant nearly two years in my backyard, sprouts a single perfect pink and white rose about three feet off the ground. When I bend over to smell it, it smells orangey, musky, and mustardy. A rose smells–well, like a rose, right? Not this one. I cut the stem six inches below the flower, bringing it up to my nose, taking three deep breaths and it still has the scent I describe. I bring the rose into the house and lay it flat on the piano next to Linda's urn. Returning four hours later, I go over to smell it and it now has no smell whatsoever.

The following morning, I pick up the rose and it is as soft and perfect as the day before. When I lift it up to smell it, it smells like a rose!

♥♥♥

On July 27th, I meet Jeannie for another session with Linda. As soon as the session commences, Linda is in the suite as a three-year-old girl wearing a red dress with white polka dots, a white ruffled collar, red and white ribbons in her hair, white leotards and white shoes.

*Linda in Christmas dress at three years old*
*(I came across this photo in Linda's photo album two days later)*

Jeannie speaks, "Linda wants to take you to an extraordinary location. There is going to be a healing honoring you." Linda explains, "Feel compassion for yourself and stay in it. Mother Mary is here surrounding you with angels and wants to heal your right leg." (I often have pain in my right hip which radiates down my leg.) Jeannie anoints my forehead with a special oil, puts her hands over my heart, and my right leg then pulsates. Mary and the angels are singing "Amazing Grace;" the music of many tongues praying over me saying, "Thy will be done."

Jeannie discloses, "Mother Mary is expressing her concern over the future of humanity which is being harmed by judgments placed upon it. There will be natural disasters in 2012 and 2013, but, because so many show their faithfulness and indulgence to her, a new beginning shall occur."

Linda affirms, "Mary wants you to continue to heal and do your work." I ask Mary how I can serve her best. She decrees, "Honor me. The souls of you and Linda are truly one." I reply to Mary, "My heart is humbled by your visitation." Linda then asks, "Dad, put a picture of me up on the mantel, the one with my arms outstretched, happy and alive. Also place a picture of Annie adjoining me. Annie is pure and is making a collage for you."

*Linda, 17 years old, in Toon Town at Universal Studios, Florida*
*(This is the photo which I found that Linda wanted on the mantle)*

♥♥♥

Unbeknownst to me, Susan's daughter Annie had been making a 30" x 40" collage of Linda. She presents it to me on August 22nd. I place it in my bedroom, propping it against the front of my bureau. I sit down and begin to pine. Linda comes behind me over my left shoulder, comforting me by resting her hand there, her touch gentle and loving.

♥♥♥

Being human, I am plagued by the injustices inflicted upon Linda. I am guided by her to the Long Island office of Three Arms Energy Balancing in Garden City, where I meet Harriette McDonough. Harriette is a gifted healer, a spiritual warrior, blessed with qualities of deep compassion, boundless devotedness and wisdom.

By accessing paramount levels in the conscious state, she ordains her clients to move lower energy out, clearing old patterns, permitting emotional freedom and sacramental healing to occur. Harriette intuitively teaches me the Emotional Freedom Technique (EFT) method of clearing energy through 14 Meridian Points (major energy pathways containing release points).

She also works with my Heart and Throat Chakras, releasing my grief, doubt, anger, depression, and sorrow brought about by Linda's transition. Once these energies move out, I cry and experience the energy of my higher self, moving into a majestic intonation of inner peace and absolute serenity.

One particular session with Harriette, on August 25th, is key to Linda's work with me. This session discloses the inner truths endowed to me through Linda, my teacher, emancipating me from repetitions of Earthly Life Cycles.

Linda calls all the angels, guides, masters, Christ, Mother Mary, Michael the

Archangel, all of my ancestors, and my simultaneous parallel lives. I vibrate into a superior spiritual self, hovering two feet above my temporal form. A blinding white force works on me; a vitality engulfs and protects me from the heavens to the Earth's core.

Harriette asks me to produce a symbol of the darkness representing the doctor who causes irreversible and eventually fatal harm to my daughter, and raise it up for all to heed. Linda asserts, "He knows you are on to him and works frantically to engulf you in evil and hatred." Immediately, a swastika appears with twisted steel cables attached to my Root, Heart, Throat, and Third Eye Chakras. The angels severe these cables and the swastika explodes into billions of particles. I am then surrounded by an illumination of three distinct columns: inner white, middle violet, and outer steel blue.

Harriette announces, "All darkness and negativity are forever blocked from you. Seal in his loathing, protecting others from harm. The shield you affix around him must remain there." I rise high above him, shrinking him into oblivion.

My current higher self then expands and leaves and a new advanced essence emerges, a combination of male and female dynamism, encompassing both myself and Linda.

Upon regarding this, Harriette pronounces, "You and Linda are twin souls, joined as one. She is truly within you and you in her." (This was also acknowledged by Mother Mary, Jeannie, and by Karen during my Lifeline Program.)

Thanks to Linda, who continues to vibrate in the highest absoluteness, I am forever absolved from further earthly incarnations. Linda bestows upon Harriette and me a tribute in this spiritual state: a jewelry box filled with trinkets of gold inside, a symbol of the recognition of our precious work together.

# Live, Laugh, Love

One morning in early September, I have an OBE . . . LINDA APPEARS TO ME, "DAD, ONCE A SOUL ATTAINS THE HIGHEST LEVEL, IT IS BATHED IN PERFECT CONTENTMENT, INFINITE LAUGHTER, PURE JOY, TRUE PEACEFULNESS, AND BLISS. LET OTHERS KNOW WE WANT THEM TO ENJOY THEIR LIVES, TO LAUGH AND HAVE FUN; SHARING THE ESSENTIAL GIFT OF HUMOR, A GIFT ONLY BESTOWED UPON HUMANS.

"HUMOR EMPOWERS US TO GROW IN SPIRIT AND MANY BEINGS WANT TO BECOME HUMAN BECAUSE OF OUR LEVITY. THE JOY OF TRANSFORMATION AND LEARNING IS MUCH GREATER THAN SORROW, MISFORTUNE, AND TRAGEDY, AND LIFTS THE VEIL BEYOND THE SADNESS.

"CHILDREN WANT THEIR PARENTS TO DELIGHT AND ENJOY. LIVING, LAUGHING, AND LOVING MAKES US JUBILANT, RELEASING JUDGMENT. IT ALLOWS US TO VIBRATE IN THE LIGHT, TO HEAL YOUR HEARTS AND LIVE INSIDE YOU. GIVING PARENTS THE PERMISSION TO BE JOVIAL AND HAPPY DISSOLVES THE FINALITY, THE FEAR OF MORTALITY.

"YOU HAVE BEEN BLESSED WITH A TREMENDOUS TALENT, YOUR SENSE OF HUMOR, AND SO HAVE I. WRITE ABOUT THE LIGHTNESS OF OUR TRAVELS TOGETHER. EVERYONE APPRECIATES THE CLASS CLOWN, THE COMEDIAN BY THE WATER COOLER. THERE IS HAPPINESS IN TRANSITION. IT IS THE TRUE MEANING OF OUR EVOLVEMENT."

INSTANTANEOUSLY, I AM TAKEN TO A MOVIE THEATRE IN 1979, WATCHING THE *THE*

CHAMP. WHEN JON VOIGHT DIES IN THE LOCKER ROOM AND RICKY SCHRODER TELLS HIM TO WAKE UP, THE ENTIRE MOVIE THEATRE ERUPTS INTO AN HYSTERICAL CRYING FIT. HUNDREDS OF PEOPLE CRY IN SYNCHRONY (THE SADDEST MOVIE EVER?). LINDA EMPOWERS ME TO RECALL MY ACTIONS, THOUGHTS, AND FEELINGS AT THAT EXACT MOMENT; CLOSING MY EYES IN THE THEATRE, I HEAR HYSTERICAL LAUGHTER.

IT OCCURS TO ME THE SAME SOUND IS EMOTED BY TWO DIRECTLY OPPOSITE EMOTIONAL RESPONSES. LINDA REVEALS SHE WANTS ME TO EXPERIENCE AGAIN THE SAME PHYSIOLOGICAL ENDORPHINS RELEASED VIA THE BRAIN FOR BOTH THESE EMOTIONAL RESPONSES. "DAD IT IS OKAY TO CRY. IT IS OKAY TO LAUGH. TO BE MERRY IS GOOD. IT'S GREAT. IT'S NORMAL. NO GUILT. JUST HAPPINESS." . . .

I comprehend exactly what Linda wants. After all, she is the ghostwriter of the book!

♥♥♥

When working with messages from the other side, we sometimes receive information all at once. This ball of information filters down into the consciousness of the medium, or the person who is experiencing a meditative state or an OBE. The symbols and examples presented are those relevant to the era on this side when we receive them.

So one of the frivolous adventures Linda and I have together is during our sessions with Jeannie in late August and early September 2012. I am a little boy, Linda a little girl. She is holding my hand as we walk on the Yellow Brick Road from *The Wizard of Oz*. We are skipping along, listening to the magical sounds, observing the red poppies in the field, savoring the sweetness of this enchanted land. Linda is my older sister, telling my younger self, "Your path will be easier now on the Yellow Brick Road." She hugs me with tenderness, caressing my hair.

I acknowledge and understand what she means.

I grow older and stronger while we walk, yet I remain humble. Linda hands me a yellow rose and a hummingbird flies by. She says, "Pay tribute to hummingbirds by putting a feeder in your yard."

As we near the Emerald City, a treasure chest of gold coins lies at our feet. Linda proclaims, "You shall be given an appropriation of money soon. You will be privileged to leave your body at your transfiguration with the wind as it passes through you." I interject, "Cool, fantastic."

♥♥♥

While on vacation in Laguna Beach, California, in March 2013, Susan and I have breakfast every morning at The Beach House. We sit outside at the same table on the balcony overlooking the water. The restaurant is built on rocks a good 30 feet above the beach.

On our last morning, a lone hummingbird flies up and hovers in front of us. All the waitresses come out, many having worked there for years. They all marvel at this site, having never seen a hummingbird on the balcony previous to this.

♥♥♥

I visit Jeannie in late September. (Once again, there is no time or space on the other side, so all communication and experience with Linda or your loved ones happens in the present.) Jeannie verbalizes, "Linda is showing me a beach and she is packing a little suitcase." I remark, "I'm going to Sanibel Island next week with my friend Mike." Jeannie responds, "Linda is also going. You will have an enlightened, healing, festive week. She'll send you a sign through your alarm clock."

Linda acknowledges, "I can experience through you by seeing with your eyes, tasting what you taste, smelling what you smell, hearing what you hear, responding physically and emotionally. I do this when you look at the photos on your computer of your trips to Italy. I enjoy all your memories and sensations on your vacations as there is no separation on the other side." I leave Jeannie excited and energized, resembling a child who can't wait to go on a trip.

Mike and I spend six days at my condo on Sanibel Island commencing on Sunday, September 30th. Every morning a beautiful monarch butterfly flies in front of us as we make our way to the beach. It accompanies us one quarter of a mile along the shore and then flies off.

When we return from our walks, another monarch butterfly accompanies us back to the condo, hovering over the lanai on the second floor. Every evening I check all the clocks, making sure they all read the same time and no other guests have left an alarm timer on.

Tuesday evening, the moon past full, the stars shining through the evening clouds, Linda is walking alongside me on the beach with Mike. Returning to the condo, I say, "Check the clocks once more." All the clocks are plugged in and all display the same time. The air conditioner is on, too.

On Wednesday morning, when I wake up, my alarm clock in my bedroom reads 9:20 AM. It seems odd because by 9:00 AM, Mike and I are usually strolling on the beach. When I walk into the kitchen, both the battery operated clock in the kitchen and the clock on the electric stove read 10:20 AM. Mike jokes, "Yeah, you finally got up. It's almost 10:30." I summon Mike to my bedroom, "Check the time on my clock." It is now reads 9:22 AM.

We check all the other clocks and every one reads 10:22 AM. If we lost power during the night and each clock has a battery back-up, it still wouldn't explain the fact that all of the other clocks are exactly one hour ahead of my electric bedroom clock, and the electric stove clock isn't flashing 12:00 to be reset.

And what about the battery clock in the kitchen? It is also one hour ahead of my bedroom clock. If the battery in that clock is dying, that clock would read a totally different time altogether!

We sit down for breakfast on the lanai. Both Mike and I have an iPhone. Everyone who has a smart phone knows it takes a minimum of three swipes to open an app. Our phones are at least three feet away.

All of a sudden, the Pandora music app on Mike's phone starts up; Diana Ross is singing, then Barbra Streisand. I see Linda by Mike's phone laughing her signature laugh. That practical joker! She purposely turns on his phone. Mike stares at me saying, "That's your daughter. I believe the clocks now." Never before or since does this happen to Mike's iPhone.

Thursday we rent a boat out of Captiva Island and go up to Cabbage Key for lunch. Linda is on the boat appreciating the breeze, watching the dolphins jump out of the water. I have been coming here 16 years. It's a tradition to tape a dollar bill with your name on it to a door, wall, or ceiling as sailors did centuries long ago.

I tape mine exactly three feet off the ground on the wall behind the main dining room doors after writing Mike's and my names, as well as Linda's on the bill. No one ever places a dollar bill there where it is so hard to reach, so out of the way. (When Susan and I return in January 2013, the bill is gone. When I return with my cousin Charlie in May 2013, the bill is exactly where I had placed it, clearly out in the open for all to peruse. There are no tape markings over the bill suggesting someone covered it up.)

On our last morning walk on the beach, Linda holds my hand, "Behold Mike as the loving, caring, loyal friend he is." When we near the condo Linda continues, "Put your feet in the water so I can feel the ocean through you."

I walk in the water. She is five years old in her bathing suit, wet with the piquancy of the sea. We stand there as the waves converge over our feet and ankles. Linda is alive, exuberant, very content in me and next to me. She is in the light allowing me to exist in both realities simultaneously. Linda exclaims, "Thank you for a wonderful week in Sanibel!" I weep in gratification.

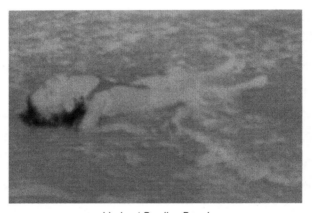

*Linda at Bradley Beach*

My communication with Linda is genuine, consistent, everyday, and matter-of-fact. We do fun things together. When I ride my bike in the park, she sometimes enters my body.

One particular ride on October 20th brings us to Hempstead Lake. She asks me to stop by the lake and walk down to the water's edge to take in the beauty of creation: the fall breeze blowing across the lake, the leaves in full autumn bloom, the white clouds rolling along the powder blue sky, the choir of birds singing.

All at once, I shift into an OBE . . . LINDA ALLOWS ME TO EXPERIENCE HER EXULTATION WHEN SHE IS HORSEBACK RIDING AT NINE YEARS OLD. WHEN LINDA MOUNTS A

HORSE, THE HORSE SUBMITS TO HER GENTLENESS, HER DETERMINATION; ALMOST AS IF THEY READ EACH OTHER'S MINDS. LINDA EXUDES CONFIDENCE RIDING THESE GIANT BEINGS WITH POISE AND GRACE.

A HUMID, SUMMER MORNING DAWNS IN AUGUST. LINDA AND I ARE SIGNED UP FOR THE 10:00 AM ADVANCED TRAIL AT PINEGROVE DUDE RANCH IN THE CATSKILL MOUNTAINS IN NEW YORK. LINDA GETS UP AT 7:00 AM KNOWING THIS IS HER BIG DAY, BUT SHE IS CONFIDENT AND MATTER-OF-FACT AT BREAKFAST.

WHEN WE REACH THE CORRAL, DEBBIE, THE CORRAL MASTER, TAKES A LOOK AT LINDA AND COMMENTS, "YOU ARE TOO SMALL TO RIDE THE ADVANCE TRAIL AMONG THE ADULTS. YOU CAN RIDE THE INTERMEDIATE TRAIL WITH THE OTHER CHILDREN."

LINDA RISES UP TO THE CHALLENGE, EYEBALLING DEBBIE, "PUT ME ON YOUR BIGGEST AND BEST HORSE AND I'LL SHOW YOU WHAT I CAN DO." DEBBIE SADDLES UP BUCKLEY, AN EIGHT-YEAR-OLD QUARTER HORSE, WHOSE NAME SPEAKS FOR ITSELF.

LINDA EMERGES FROM THE STABLE, HER RIDING BOOTS AND HELMET NEATLY SECURED, AND CLIMBS ON A BOX TO MOUNT BUCKLEY. LINDA GIVES HIM THREE HARD SWIFT KICKS AND YELLS, "GIDDY-YAP!" BUCKLEY TAKES OFF AT A FULL GALLOP AROUND THE CORRAL. LINDA IS LEANING FORWARD LIKE A JOCKEY AT THE KENTUCKY DERBY. SHE TURNS HIM, STOPS HIM, BRINGS HIM TO A CANTOR, THEN A TROT, TURNS HIM AGAIN, KICKS HIM AND BUCKLEY IS BACK TO A GALLOP. THEN SHE PULLS UP ON THE REIGNS, SLOWS HIM TO A WALK, STARES AT DEBBIE AND SAYS, "SO, WHAT DO YOU THINK NOW?" DEBBIE EMOTES THE BIGGEST HOWL AND REPLIES, "PUT THIS ONE ON THE ADULT ADVANCE TRAIL."

LINDA IS GRINNING FROM EAR TO EAR, ACCOMPLISHING WHAT SHE SET OUT TO DO. SHE RIDES BUCKLEY THE ENTIRE WEEK AND I EXPERIENCE HER EXHILARATION . . .

*Linda and Buckley at Pinegrove Dude Ranch*

On November 10th, Linda shows Jeannie the condo complex at the beach, the tennis courts to the right, exactly as it appears. What she then reveals to Jeannie blows me away: "I change the clock in my father's bedroom so he can have an extra hour of sleep and I turn on Mike's iPhone. I am beside my father night and day, sending the monarch butterflies to him, sitting on the boat, holding his hand in the water in front of the condo."

My cousin Angela asks me for a sign from Linda. Jeannie imparts, "Linda is in an azure dress at a party. At the party, look for three signs: a flickering of lights, a white feather, and a rainbow on the ground."

♥♥♥

On Saturday, January 5th, 2013, we are at a party celebrating my Aunt Marilyn's 80th birthday at Angela's house. Linda and my aunt are extremely fond of each other during Linda's physical sojourn.

Throughout the entire party, all of Angela's second floor lights flicker. Angela has never had any electrical problems in the 25 years she has been living there, nor any problems since. A fire pit, constructed in her yard for the party, burns brightly during the night, the flames emanating the colors of the rainbow. As we are leaving the party Angela calls to me, "I found this white feather on one of my down throw pillows. Linda is here!"

# Thanksgiving 2012

Keep in mind, children and loved ones communicate with us in various ways, all of which are normal and natural. Every way is the right way and no one can claim they have a special or superior method. The key here is to trust your knowing and your experience, and understand that any form of contact is real, true, and part of your essential birthright. We are all eternal beings, unique in character, yet one in love. Let us be thankful for allowing ourselves to be open to touch, feel, and acknowledge our teachers, our children in the light.

♥♥♥

On the Saturday after Thanksgiving, I drive Susan and Annie to Kennedy Airport. They are going to Anthem, Arizona, to visit Susan's sister Joann. As I am returning home I begin feeling forlorn and start to lament. Linda manifests saying, "Dad, it shall be you and me. We'll enjoy ourselves and you won't be in despair when we get back to the house."

While riding my exercise bike that evening, Linda nudges me, "Let's go in the hot tub." When I remove the hot tub cover the temperature reads 101°, but it is always set at 99°. "Surprise!" exclaims Linda, "I set the hot tub to 101°. It is very cold and windy tonight and I want you nice and warm." She is right for I am very comfortable.

As the winds grows stronger, the branches on the tree above the hot tub shake violently, a vibration initiates within me and Linda acknowledges, "You have free will and you can pass with the wind, but you choose to stay. Savor the rest of your continuance for you have broken through the illusion of earthly circumstances. When you cry for me, you cry for everyone whose child passes because you embrace it in your heart, your compassion is pure." (The following morning when I lift the cover of the hot tub to add chemicals, the temperature reads 99°. I didn't adjust any of the controls the night before.)

Later while having dinner, Linda and I watch *Dolphin Tale*. Linda tells me, "You can work with disabled children using Hemi-Sync from The Monroe Institute to teach them to separate out of their bodies so they can explore the physical and non-physical world, play, run, and have fun. I shall be there with Aunt Terry to help you."

On Sunday, I fire up the new wood burning stove in the dining room. The whole house is filled with the incense of oak. I pull over the rocker from the living room tumbling into an OBE . . . LINDA APPEARS, "GO BACK TO THE DEN IN OLD BRIDGE." ONCE THERE, WE ARE PUTTING UP A CHRISTMAS TREE, DECORATING IT WITH BULBS AND ORNAMENTS, SMELLING THE FRESHNESS OF PINE NEEDLES, OUR FAVORITE CHRISTMAS CDS PLAYING ON THE STEREO; THE FIREPLACE ROARING. WE POSITION ICICLE BULBS ACROSS THE MANTEL AND LINDA HELPS ME DECORATE THE WINDOWS IN HER BEDROOM.

RETURNING TO THE DEN WITH POPCORN IN HAND, I SIT IN THE RECLINER AND SHE LIES ON THE COUCH WHILE I ARRANGE THE PILLOWS AND THE MINNIE MOUSE BLANKET THE WAY SHE TREASURES IT. LINDA SHARES A COMPLIMENT, "WHY DOES YOUR POPCORN TASTE THE BEST?" I REPLY, "I SPRINKLE A LOT OF FAIRY DUST ON IT." "YOU'VE BEEN WATCHING TOO

MANY CARTOONS LATELY," SHE BANTERS WHILE GIVING ME A BIG HUG AND A KISS.

WE WATCH MOVIES TOGETHER: *NEWSIES, LITTLE MERMAID, BEAUTY AND THE BEAST, HOLIDAY INN, WHITE CHRISTMAS.* WE DANCE TO OUR SONG AND I DO MY IMITATION OF BING CROSBY AND DANNY KAYE SINGING "SISTERS, SISTERS." SHE ENUNCIATES, "I CHERISH THE WAY YOU DECORATE THE HOUSE FOR CHRISTMAS, SO CHEERFUL AND FESTIVE. THE WEEKENDS NEVER COME FAST ENOUGH AND I'M ALWAYS GETTING CAUGHT DAY-DREAMING BY MY TEACHER. DAD, YOU ARE A GOOD FATHER AND YOU SPOIL ME WITH A LOT OF TOYS. I REALLY BELIEVE IN SANTA CLAUS BECAUSE OF YOU."

LINDA GLOWS LIKE A VIBRANT STAR. SHE IS NO PARTICULAR AGE, FIRST 7, THEN 12, THEN 20 . . .

*Linda and Santa*

On December 8th, I have a session with Jeannie. "Linda wants you to play alongside her as two little children so your inner child can be carefree." I ask Jeannie if Linda sees my mother. Linda nods, "Your mother is holding my hand

and she is a good grandmother. We all choose to leave: your mother, Terry, and I. You help many, many souls cross to the other side. You shall be in the light when you make your transition, something which you could have done in the hot tub while the wind was lifting you up, but you choose to stay to finish your work. I know exactly how you like the temperature in the hot tub on cold nights."

Linda asks Jeannie if she can help treat Jeannie's next client. Linda often accompanies Jeannie to healing groups, prayer groups, the Ramtha School; and when Jeannie meets her own personal psychic and healer, Franz.

As Jeannie walks me out, I pass the young woman envisioning why Linda wants to stay and help Jeannie do a healing.

# Christmas 2012

The First Christmas, or the first holiday season when we gather to celebrate and exchange gifts after a loved one passes, is the most difficult one, especially if the loved one is our child. It is the time of year when people gather together, expressing benevolence, experiencing boundless joy, sharing heartfelt emotions amongst family and friends. But for us, it magnifies the loss, the sorrow, the void, the heartbreak, the loneliness, the grief, the dejection. We become overwhelmed with sadness, pain, and tears.

Even though I have been given many gifts by Linda, blessed with the knowing we all exist eternally, I am still human; "If you prick us, do we not bleed?" I can't listen to any Christmas songs, having to change the radio station in the office; bawling uncontrollably and incessantly when I stare at pictures of Linda or even think of her. I still haven't played the piano or picked up a paint brush, nor can I look at Christmas cards or wish anyone a Merry Christmas.

There are no holiday office parties, no social gatherings for me. Some friends and family stay away, as if I have the plague and they will catch it. They are uncomfortable in themselves, fearing my anguish will infect them, ruin their holiday spirit; they are afraid of the illusion of the finality of their own mortality.

However many, many loving people do embrace me, comfort me, call me, and Linda and I are forever grateful considering their devotion and support. But I welcome the grief because I am cognizant and it is an integral part of the healing process.

What I learn from Linda, if you silence your inner judge, you experience the true essence of courage that allows the heartache, loss, loneliness, and grief to be just what they are, nothing more. Silencing the inner judge removes the anger -- the opposite of which is depression. You feel the pain of separation, but the fear of it controlling you is gone. It is normal to permit these emotions to envelop you. It's okay to cry in public, at the dinner table, or a party. You can live by virtue of not allowing your superego to cast judgment or guilt on how you are perceived by yourself or others. An excellent book that works in this realm is *Soul without Shame,* by Byron Brown.

Give yourself permission to seek counseling through individual therapy or share your feelings in bereavement groups. It's okay to take medication whether herbal or prescription, utilizing what is available to help you heal. We have been though an unimaginable tragedy!

Remember, our children want us to live, laugh, and love. They courageously fulfill their promise to us, inspiring us to examine what life is; a place to evolve, learn, and grow. We in turn honor their courage, their memory by living! As Clarence, the guardian angel, in *It's a Wonderful Life* says to George Bailey, "You've been given a great gift, George. Don't you see what a terrible thing it would be to throw it all away?"

Our children, our teachers, our angels, our guides, our treasures, our blessings, inspire us. They give us the greatest of Christmas gifts, themselves! We can't throw it all away! At the end of the movie, George cries out on the snowy bridge, "I want to live God. Please let me live." This is what our children, our loved ones, want us to do, live as best we can.

On December 22nd, I meet Jeannie asking Linda if the exhilaration on the other side is different for the holidays. Linda declares, "It's always Christmas here. We are all children darting and playing about. It is The North Pole of Eden; trees of all sizes, shapes, and colors adorned with candy canes, ornaments, packages wrapped in kaleidoscopes, glowing splendor of snow falling, abundant toys, angels, fairies, elves, animals, birds of all kinds and rainbow flowers. It is ecstasy, fantasy, and actuality all in one. We are orbs of pure scintillation, radiance, and adoration. You shall not be heavy-hearted this Christmas. There are guides and masters who want to work on the back of your neck, an intense unfolding will commence." Immediately enormous expansion and bliss overtake me.

Linda continues, "I shall be within you when you watch *White Christmas*. Look for me on the sled at the end of the movie." I ask her, "Which Christmas videos of you do you want me to watch?" She replies, "You'll decide which ones; they are all full of beautiful memories seeing I am alive in all the videos."

♥♥♥

I am in my den on Long Island courageously watching videos of Linda at Christmastime and the holiday movies she and I watched together on Christmases past. Linda manifests around me, a glowing star of brilliance and brightness, clutching my arm as we watch *White Christmas* and Christmas home video from 1988, 1990, and 2004, when we dance to "The Best Things Happen While You're Dancing." I emote tears of jubilation and heartache; elated that I have all of these moments on film and comforted through her touch as she surrounds me from the ethereal. I close my eyes.

. . . A FLICKER OCCURS, AN OBE INITIATES AND I ENTER MY APARTMENT IN BROOKLYN.

LINDA IS SEVEN MONTHS OLD DONNING A RED DRESS WITH WHITE LEOTARDS AND I AM HOLDING HER. THERE IS AN AIR OF REVERENCE SURROUNDING HER; THE LIGHTS ON THE CHRISTMAS TREE SHIMMER. THE AROMA OF BAKED COOKIES, A HEARTY TOMATO SAUCE, A ROAST COOKING IN THE OVEN FILL THE AIR. THE BELL RINGS AND THE LANDLORD ENTERS DRESSED AS SANTA CLAUS. LINDA DOESN'T DISCERN WHAT TO MAKE OF THIS JOLLY FELLOW IN THE PADDED RED SUIT, RED HAT, WHITE BEARD, AND BLACK BELT. TRUSTING EYES FOLLOW ME AS I HAND LINDA OVER TO HIM; THE ENCHANTMENT OF AN INFANT LOOKING AT OLD ST. NICK. "OH, HOW ADORABLE. QUICK, GET THE CAMERA!"

WE ALL TAKE TURNS PHOTOGRAPHING OUR IMAGINARY CHILDHOOD HERO WITH LINDA WHO IS OBLIVIOUS TO ALL THE EXCITEMENT. "WHAT'S ALL THE FUSS?" SHE IS PROBABLY SAYING TO HERSELF. I RECEIVE THE GREATEST CHRISTMAS THRILL—WATCHING SANTA HOLD LINDA FOR THE VERY FIRST TIME . . .

♥♥♥

Keeping to her word, I am not sad on Christmas Day. Susan and I fly to Clearwater Beach, Florida, to spend Christmas with all of Susan's family. My father-in-law, Joe made his transition in March 2012 and my mother-in-law, Terry wants the whole family together to celebrate the accomplishments of a great man, and, to her credit, she keeps the spirit of Christmas and Dad alive the whole week.

While opening boxes Christmas night, Susan perceives a shadow pass over her into her parents' bedroom. After dinner, while playing cards in the dining room, we all remark that he is near us and I can hear his laughter as Mom lays her cards on the table and cries out, "Gin Rummy!"

Some of the family, including Susan and myself, spend December 26th and 27th at Walt Disney World, staying in the Animal Kingdom. From childhood, Linda always enjoys a Disney vacation. She is with us on The Great Movie Ride,

Tower of Terror, Muppet 3D, Ellen's Energy Adventure, and in the 50's PrimeTime Café at Disney's Hollywood Studios. Linda walks with me and Susan in the World Showcase and waits in line with us at Thunder Mountain, Splash Mountain, Space Mountain, Haunted Mansion, and Pirates of the Caribbean.

Since most of these rides are at night, Linda appears as an adult, clowning and carousing. Once again, by working through the sadness, the veneer lifts and I can see and experience Linda next to me; presenting herself alive, existing simultaneously on all planes.

On December 29th, the whole family goes to Serenity Gardens in Largo, Florida, for a ceremony placing Dad's ashes in a stone bench near the edge of the lake. On this beautiful, sunny morning my nephew Joseph plays Dad's favorite song, "Take Me Out to the Ball Game," on the ukulele while we all sing along. I remain behind a while because Dad is sitting on his bench smoking a cigar with Linda by his side. The following day I feel Linda and Dad inside of me as we stroll down to the beach holding hands; the wind gently caressing my face.

Back home on Long Island for New Year's Eve, I watch two videos as Linda rests beside me in my den. In the first, I am ushering in the New Year holding a newborn child. The second one is from 2002, when I have a party for Linda, her friends Ali, Lauren, and Kelly, and Linda's boyfriend Roger. Susan is also in this video. Linda in her usual way keeps us all bemused telling stories, imitating her teachers and friends including mannerisms and facial expressions. It is a great way to bring in 2013.

# Everyday Life 2013

What is everyday life: an oxymoron? a paradox? It is the attempt by us to make sense of our existence without our children or loved ones. For me, I think of the entertaining things I did to make Linda crack-up, those remarkable times we shared.

Slowly, painfully, I begin playing the songs on the piano she likes best: "Can You Feel the Love Tonight," "Yesterday," "The Way We Were," "New York State of Mind," and "Like A Prayer." The more I play, the more she sits on my lap smiling, the more I feel happiness while I cry. I attempt to paint, but my concentration level isn't there.

Turning to television, I view shows we watch together when she is six years old: *I Love Lucy* and *The Golden Girls*. Playing more Madonna, Cher, and Streisand on my stereo, the music and liveliness fills my home, allowing my heart to beat again.

Pulling out old photos, I talk to them -- "Remember when one of your training wheels got stuck in the hole in the street and you pedaled and laughed." "Boy, the principal was really pissed when I showed up playing baseball with your class during lunch break." "I can still hear the crack of the bat when you hit that home run to win the game."

Replaying hours of videos of her chronologically, I embrace solace and recognition; reliving the pilgrimage of a blessed cherub who came to Earth and filled my subsistence with exuberance and inspiration. I find a note I wrote to her when she started kindergarten:

### Dear Linda

*I love you. You are my best friend.*
*I like when you come over for the weekend.*
*We have a lot of fun.*
*I like to go on vacations with you.*
*I like to play with you and Greg.*
*I hope you have a lot fun with your*
*friends at school.*

### I Love You
### Dad

On January 12th, I meet with Jeannie. Smelling cigar smoke, she describes a tall man with grey hair and a big smile. "This is Susan's father, a humble man who raises a family, idolizes and deeply loves his wife and children, and is very proud of them. He delights walking with you and Linda on the beach, thanking you for sitting by the lake when the others left, and for marrying Susan. It is he she notices Christmas night and he wants to shake your hand." Our hands touch; the energy gentle, genuine, and comforting.

Jeannie then verbalizes, "I want to express gratitude to Linda for bringing Joe to our session." (I hadn't told Jeannie Susan's father's name.) She continues, "Linda thanks you for a spectacular vacation in Walt Disney World."

88

♥♥♥

On January 26th, Linda asks me to write about this particular session with Jeannie. Linda enunciates, "People need to understand they aren't alone. The same thing that happens to you because of the work you do with me shall happen to others if they are willing to do the work, too."

Linda shows Jeannie a clean slate, "There shall be a miracle here." Linda asks the Holy Spirit and all the guides to create an aperture of sanctity; a dimension on the other side, similar to an NDE, endorsing initiation and growth.

I arrive at an Indian village as a decorated warrior, yet wounded, and I am told to walk through fire, yet I do not burn. Linda explains, "You need to incinerate the illusions of the material world." Surrounded in a cocoon of blue and orange luminosity, I grow larger, the illusions of embodiment melt away as voices sing, "Come, Holy Ghost, Creator Blest."

Linda appears as a little girl, in her pink snowsuit, pink hood, pink and white snow boots, and white glitter gloves. She is making snow angels, sliding her arms and legs back and forth. "Come on, Dad, lie down and make angels, too." She grabs my hand and I am catapulted back to when I am young boy sitting in church. Linda shows me the gifts my mother gives me, inspiring my devotion to God, Mother Mary, and Jesus.

A hand reaches out to embrace me. It is the Hand of God and I weep incessantly. A voice all-knowing, all-loving breathes, "WHAT I DO FOR YOU, I DO FOR ALL."

♥♥♥

My mother, as we were growing up, instilled in us respect towards all religions, races, and creeds. She taught that spirituality is a freedom, a development, a process. "Religion is grammar school," she would tell us. "It is the basic foundation upon which we evolve into deeper universal truths, knowledge, and wholeness. We are all bound as one."

Even though I was reared Catholic, I don't prescribe to any one religion. I incorporate equally all teachings, all beliefs into my knowing. Every belief system is beautiful, special, noteworthy, holy, and sacred. It is these teachings our guides use to stimulate us to seek a greater vibration.

I remember one summer I went to every different house of worship for services: a mosque, a synagogue, a Buddhist temple, Lutheran, Episcopal, Methodist, Baptist, Mormon, and Greek Orthodox churches. I read books on Taoism, Hinduism, and Sufism. What amazes me most is that in all religions people experience the same message when they connect to their inner purpose: unconditional love! I have been honored to treat patients from all walks of life and it is the same love, gratitude, and appreciation they bestow upon me.

♥♥♥

. . . I WAKE UP TO AN OBE ON VALENTINE'S DAY. LINDA, ALMOST FIVE YEARS OLD, GREETS ME WITH "HAPPY VALENTINE'S DAY," CARRYING BALLOONS OF ALL SIZES, SHAPES, AND COLORS. SHE HANDS ME A WHITE, STUFFED TEDDY BEAR WITH A BEATING HEART, A BEAUTIFUL BOUQUET OF PINK ROSES, AND A BOX OF CHOCOLATES SHAPED LIKE LIPS. I OPEN THE BOX AND BITE INTO ONE OF THE PIECES, DELIGHTING IN THIS LITTLE ESSENCE OF HEAVEN. SHE PUTS HER TINY HANDS IN MINE AS I BEND DOWN AND PICK HER UP. LAUGHING HER CONTAGIOUS LAUGH, SHE CARESSES MY CHEEKS, KISSING ME EVER SO SOFTLY; OUR ENERGIES JOIN AS ONE AND IT ENVELOPS MY ENTIRE SUBSTANCE.

LINDA DELICATELY ARTICULATES IN MY EAR, "ISN'T THIS MUCH BETTER THAN A CARD

OR PHONE CALL. I AM BESIDE YOU ALL DAY, MY FUNNY VALENTINE." . . .

♥♥♥

Linda is able to manifest in the everyday. Souls in infiniteness can move energy and matter. Here are a few examples so you can see what is truly commonplace, ordinary, normal, and real.

Linda worked many summers in my office during high school and college. The staff and patients knew her well as a practical joker. One day in March, she knocks over the sterilization unit in our office, witnessed by Jessica and Liz.

On another, while I am treating my patient John, accompanied by Jessica, Linda shuts down the fluorescent fixtures and equipment in the operatory that I am working in. I check the circuit breakers, every one is on; the other four operatories and the rest of the office continue to function normally. She does this in front of John because he is unobstructed to the continuity of consciousness, possessing the natural ability to contact the other side.

When I return to the operatory, John orates, "It's your daughter, Linda." With that, everything functions again. In the 20 years I have been practicing in my office, this problem never occurs prior to this incident or since.

On March 27th, while working at my computer on the third floor in my home, I notice papers rustling on the floor behind me. When I turn, a shadow walks past me. I call down to Susan, "Where are the cats?" She shouts, "They are in the basement and the door is closed. Why do you ask?" "It's the boss," I retort. "She is walking by me."

In April, Liz enters the restroom next to my office. When she enters the restroom the office lights are on. When she exists, they are off. Later that same morning, I am standing next to Liz while she is on the phone conversing with a patient. The speaker on the second front desk phone, seven feet from us, turns on. Once again, nothing of the sort has ever happened in my office.

On April 14th, Susan and I attend the Broadway play, *The Book of Mormon*. Our tickets are in the last row of the upper balcony; the aisle seat and the one adjoining it. At this distance, I need my glasses to view the stage clearly. I look over and there is Linda sitting on the steps to my right, pointing to my glasses, "Take them off. You will be able to see everything crystal clear and all the colors shall be vibrant and alive." I don't need my glasses the rest of the day or that evening.

Traveling home on the Long Island Railroad, the seat to my right is empty. Linda rests on my right shoulder, closes her eyes, and sleeps the entire time. She's about 13 or 14 years old.

*Linda and me at Epcot*

I wake up depressed on my birthday. As I lay in bed staring at the ceiling, my despair unbearable, Linda whispers, "Dad, take me upstairs and go through your desk, the one you still have from second grade and read all the cards you saved over the years. Feel my presence as you read them, savoring my words in your heart. My drawings shall bring a smile to your face. Then we will go into the hot tub and there I will take away your sorrow."

I do as I'm told, ascending the steps to the third floor. When I reach the top step, a singing brown birthday bear she bought for me three years prior, placed some 30 feet away, resting on built-in shelves attached to the front wall, lights up and begins singing "Happy Birthday." Stopping me in my tracks, this phenomenon lasts a full seven minutes encompassing me in pure unconditional love, jubilation, and everlasting bliss.

During this time, I rummage through my desk and find a handwritten card in multi-colored crayon in my drawer:

**FOR MY DADDY**

*This is for my daddy*
*Who's as special*
*as can be*
*It brings a wish,*
*A hug, a kiss*
*Because it comes from me!*

**HAPPY BIRTHDAY**
**XOXOXO**
**I LOVE YOU**
**LINDA**

I read cards she mailed to me from college, "Thank you for making this possible," and find simple childhood drawings of her and me driving in a car holding hands.

Later, in the hot tub, I am overwhelmed with jubilance and yes, solace, as she intertwines her emotions with mine.

That evening, I watch a video of my 31st birthday. Linda, almost three, is sitting on my lap, her endearing smile radiating from ear to ear. I see myself and say, "Can anyone really be this happy?" Her eyes are beacons of light as she blows out my birthday candles, hugging and kissing me with fervent emotion. Her face, filled with giddy excitement, explodes into an aura of wonderment, as I unwrap a stuffed rainbow unicorn about one foot high and hand it to her. "This is what you bought me for my birthday and I want you to sleep with it every night, so you can ride to the stars. What do you want to name the unicorn?" Linda replies, "Sparkle!" in her intriguing, delectable voice.

A distressing day none-the-less, I sob intermittently, but find comfort in the assurance that Linda is alive and it is irrefutable.

# Easter 2013

Linda celebrates Easter with all souls in the light. Every Easter since Linda's birth, my sister Terry would make hard-boiled eggs and color them with her. While the eggs were drying, we'd get into my car and drive to a petting zoo, where Linda would pet and feed deer, goats, lambs, rabbits, calves, chickens, ducks, swans; every animal imaginable. Then we would wait in line for a pony ride. These experiences with Terry helped to bring about Linda's love for animals, an adoration she maintains in the celestial. When we return home there would be an Easter egg hunt and surprises left from the Easter Bunny.

Easter is the only time of year when many people actually let the endowment of eternity into their hearts, lifting the veil of separation between human and divine, truly believing we live beyond our mortal subsistence. I hope what I write in this book shall permit many to comprehend that this is a normal, everyday occurrence, not a once-a-year event.

In my session with Jeannie the day before Easter Sunday, she describes Linda as a seven-year-old girl holding a wicker basket filled with pastel-colored eggs. Linda is wearing a white dress adorned with green and red flowers, white stockings, white shoes, and a white Easter bonnet with a pink ribbon. I am wearing a light grey suit with a shirt and tie.

Jeannie accounts, "Linda is happiest here with other people around her, especially children. She is holding your hand, while petting a dog, as you walk to church where she hands you yellow and green tulips."

*I found this 1992 Easter Sunday picture of Linda and me after my session with Jeannie*

As happens so often when I visit Jeannie, an OBE ensues . . . LINDA AND I ARE SHOPPING AT THE DISNEY STORE. SHE IS INFATUATED WITH THE MOVIE, *101 DALMATIANS*, AND USES THE MONEY FROM HER PIGGY BANK TO BUY THE FOLLOWING: PONGO, PERDITA, AND 6 DALMATIAN PUPPIES.

WE ARE NOW IN MY BEDROOM IN OLD BRIDGE WHERE LINDA IS TUCKING STUFFED DALMATIAN DOGS UNDER THE COVERS, PICKING ONE PUPPY TO HOLD, COUNTING ALL THE REST TO MAKE SURE THEY ARE ALL THERE UNDER THE BLANKET READY FOR SLEEP. LINDA EXCITINGLY VOICES, "DAD, THIS IS A SPECIAL NIGHT BECAUSE I AM GOING TO SLEEP WITH

ALL THE DOGS IN YOUR BIG BED. DO YOU THINK WE HAVE ENOUGH ROOM FOR EVERYBODY, EVEN MY NINJA TURTLE PILLOW?" I TURN AWAY AS I START TO SHED TEARS FROM SHEER EXHILARATION AND RESPOND, "WHY OF COURSE. WE HAVE PLENTY OF ROOM." . . .

At the end of the session, Linda proclaims to me and Jeannie, "All in heaven bestow blessings of elatedness and infinite gratitude upon those who open their hearts and minds to the celebration of Easter. We pray for godliness and purity to embrace all."

# Linda's First Birthday in the Light

Throughout the book I introduce a new language, a new way of communicating; my interactions with Linda are always in the present. When acquiring language skills before we can actually read, write, or put it all together, we memorize letters, sound out consonants and vowels, and write and enunciate simple words and phrases.

Eventually our conscious minds absorb the language; we think, speak, and verbally express our emotions and convictions and communicate with ourselves and others with this language; defining who we are in typical, average, commonplace situations.

To me, May 5th is the celebration of Linda's worldly and heavenly birthday because all lifetimes, all realities, are happening simultaneously; an unending celebration in the light. I honor her by making this day a momentous occasion, incorporating her purpose in both the physical and non-physical. Yes I am grief-stricken and there isn't a morning or evening when I don't cry. I call out yearning for her companionship, but I view her earthly years as a pilgrimage filled with wondrous memories and glorious adventures.

*If I could gather up all the smiles, laughs, memories, and pride that you brought me through the years and give them back to you, I would.*

*Maybe that way you'd understand just what it means to have a daughter like you and why you're one of the most important things in the world to me.*

*No one could ever love a daughter and believe in her more deeply than I love and believe in you.*

♥♥♥

On May 1st, I meet with Jeannie. "I am going to Sanibel to celebrate Linda's first birthday in the light and I want her with me." Jeannie affirms, "Linda fancies being a little girl with you and will sit adjoining you in the open seat on the plane holding your hand. She will walk with you on the beach at night. Take a blanket and lie under the stars for she will send you a very specific sign and you will have fun."

Linda reveals, "Other souls have gratitude toward me because I help them when they transition because of you helping me after my transition. You release a soul who does you and others harm when you are a young boy. You, and you alone, authorize him to move out of darkness, something we acknowledge on our side."

Sunday, May 5th, I arrive on Sanibel joined by my cousin Charlie who helps me set out a collage of Linda on my bedroom bureau; amazed at the intensity of Linda's presence. Included in the collage are pictures of family and friends, some of whom have made their journey to the other side. I ask Charlie if I can be alone with Linda before we go down to the beach.

. . . As I lay on my bed, I roll out of my body finding myself in Brooklyn at Linda's first birthday party; immediately joining with my 29-year-old self. Linda is standing, holding onto the kitchen cabinet, in a lavender, pink, and white

BALLOONED, RUFFLED, CHIFFON DRESS WITH MATCHING LEGGINGS, PINK AND WHITE SHOES, AND LAVENDER BOWS IN HER TINY AMOUNT OF HAIR. SHE IS LAUGHING; THE REVERBERATION OF HER WHOLE BODY CONSUMES EVERYONE AS HER HEARTINESS IGNITES OUR NEARLY 50 RELATIVES TO REMARK, "WHERE DID SHE GET THAT LAUGH FROM?"

MY FATHER PICKS HER UP AND PUTS HER ON THE TABLE, THE CANDLES ON THE BIRTHDAY CAKE LIT IN FRONT OF THEM. THE LIGHTS ARE SHUT AND THE FIRST OF MANY SHARED REPETITIONS OF "HAPPY BIRTHDAY" BEGIN, HONORING LINDA AND MY FATHER BORN ON THE SAME DAY.

THE LOUD SOUNDS IN AN ITALIAN HOUSEHOLD ARE QUITE TYPICAL; INTOXICATING, INVIGORATING, UPLIFTING, AND INSPIRING. ON THIS BIRTHDAY, THE HONOR OF BLOWING OUT LINDA'S CANDLE GOES TO MY FATHER, A ROLE THAT WILL BE PERMANENTLY REVERSED WHEN A TWO-YEAR-OLD TAKES COMMAND NEXT YEAR.

I POSITION LINDA ON MY LAP ON THE FLOOR IN FRONT OF THE LIVING ROOM SOFA; PRESENTS IN MOUNDS UP TO THE CEILING. I FIND MYSELF SIMULTANEOUSLY HOLDING LINDA AND OBSERVING THE PARTY FROM THE OPPOSITE SIDE OF THE ROOM. SHE SITS LIKE ROYALTY, HELPING ME UNRAVEL EACH PACKAGE, CLAPPING TO THE CHEERING OF "HOW CUTE," AS SHE TUGS AT HER BOXES. SHE ARTICULATES HER FIRST WORDS, "MOW, OINK, URF-URF, DA-DA," AND I COMPREHEND AND RECOGNIZE ENDEARMENT AND AFFECTION AS EACH OF MY RELATIVES REMARK, "THAT ONE'S FROM ME!" . . .

On Tuesday, one year after Linda's transition, Charlie and I ride up to Cabbage Key via boat for lunch. As I explained earlier, sailors tape dollar bills with their names on them on the ceilings, walls, posts, doors, and doorways. The establishment is packed and we notice one empty table which Charlie grabs as I go wash up.

Upon returning, sitting in the seat opposite him, he says to me, "Cuz, over your head there is a dollar bill dangling down from the ceiling." I glance upward and read, "LINDA IS MY GAL." Then I get up and locate my dollar bill on the wall exactly where I placed it in October, but can't find in January.

Wednesday evening, Charlie leaves and my friend Sanibel Mike arrives; Linda not wasting any time contacting him. At 3:15 AM, Mike calls out, "Your daughter is here because I know I shut my NOOK off prior to putting out the light and now the game Tetris is playing." I enter his bedroom, watch him turn the NOOK off and we both go back to sleep.

Fifteen minutes later, Mike enters my room waking me up, "My NOOK is on again. Tetris is going crazy!" Mike has never had an incident with his NOOK either before or since this occurrence.

Following dinner Thursday evening, Mike and I bring a blanket down to the beach and lie under the stars. It is a beautiful, clear evening. A half hour passes and we both sit up noticing a shadow walking past us 20 feet away at the water's edge. Mike exclaims, "Linda!" Who am I to disagree? This is the same shadow that passes by my computer on March 27th.

When I wake up Friday morning, I turn in my bed noticing Linda as a little girl sleeping under the covers. I am wide awake because it is 8:30 AM and I have to get up to use the bathroom.

# The Graduation Party

In May 2013, Susan sent out invitations to all of our family and friends announcing a Butterfly Releasing Ceremony, a graduation party, in honor of Linda, to be held on Sunday, June 9th.

In my session with Jeannie on May 18th, I ask Linda if she will be at the ceremony. Jeannie announces, "Yes, and those on the other side are acknowledging this as Linda's Graduation Party from the Earth Life System as well." I then experience the recognition of abounding benevolence and acclamation Linda and the other celestials have for this day.

Jeannie continues, "You finally receive your full wings, surrounded in a gold aura. Both you and Linda have on graduation caps. Linda is coming as her adult self. Falling just below her knees, her yellow dress with a white collar and three buttons down the center is accompanied by a yellow and white purse draping over her shoulder. She is handing you a yellow dandelion. This event on Earth is very rare and majestic.

"An uncle of yours is coming to the party commenting he wouldn't miss it. He is tall, very distinguished, and will be wearing a suit. When he greets you, he calls your name in a sing-song voice."

I ask Jeannie if he goes by a special name. She affirms, "You call him Tony Mars. [Uncle Tony always greeted me and all of his other nieces and nephews in the same way.] Locked in his arm is his wife, a tall, beautiful, dark-haired woman wearing a 1950s dress (my Aunt Marianne, my first messenger).

"Another uncle is coming holding a Scotch glass and his name is Sal. Your father is donning a mustache, smoking a cigar.

"A woman, very pretty and sexy, is getting my attention. She is short, with a green dress, high heels and her hair is done up." I say to Jeannie, "I have a name for her, too." Jeannie replies, "Goddess of beauty and love. She is coming with her husband and her son." (I call my Aunt Nina "Ninfa," goddess of beauty and love, whose son Joseph started me on my evolution.)

"There is a table of men playing cards at the party," Jeannie observes. "They are sitting by the bushes near the back fence and one man is remarking, 'That Frank is a good kid.' The other side experiences the party since all realities are one and inseparable."

On May 29th, at 7:00 AM, in my home on Long Island, I wake up to use the bathroom. It is a clear bright morning, with the sun shining through the windows. As I exit the bathroom, Linda walks past me in shadow form, the top of her head in line with my lips. (Linda is 4' 10" and I am 5' 6".) She walks down the steps and I follow her outside to my screened-in porch.

Resting in my rocker with Linda beside me, I meditate while listening to the birds and watching the sun as it rises up between the branches of the trees. She expresses, "It is in the early morning that we are closest to the glory of God and the wonders of creation."

Anticipating the Graduation Party, I meet Jeannie again on June 1st. Jeannie begins, "Linda is a little girl and everyone on both sides are excited about the party. With a golden crown on your head, the angels have put you on a horse by a river with Linda behind you."

When I ask Jeannie who's appearing at the party, she replies, "A huge table of men playing cards, acting as guardians, and women serving food and drink. The men will raise their heads and nod if you call out their names." So I set roll call in motion, receiving nods from the following: "My father, Uncle Joe C., Uncle Tony, Uncle Sal, Uncle Joe R., Uncle Victor, Joe M. [Susan's father], Uncle Walter, Uncle Sol, Grandpa Charlie, Grandpa Frank, Grandpa Angelo, Cousin Bob J., Cousin Nick M., Nick the painter, Al Natch, and Steve A."

Jeannie proceeds, "Women are coming forward. Your mother is here. So is Aunt Marianne. Your sister, Terry, is bringing a crumb cake. There is an older matronly woman with glasses cooking lasagna and meatballs, calling herself Lucia [Aunt Lucy]. Another older woman is bringing cannolis and goes by the name Rose [Grandma Rose]. A woman who is your godmother is coming with Tessy [Grandma Tessy], and sisters Josie and Mamie [Grandma Connie], Missy and Josephine, Chris and Cobina, Aunt Joanne and many, many friends. Bring them into your consciousness and they shall arrive."

I ask if this party will elevate the other celestials in attendance. Jeannie replies, "Linda is in the highest vibration and is very powerful. Each soul has an individual destiny as well as a collective one. Linda is showing me the souls at the party are climbing up a ladder."

I then channel Mother Mary and the Holy Spirit; a tremendous amount of heat is emitted from my Third Eye Chakra down to my hands, a deep purple hue projecting forth from my body. The Holy Spirit descends proclaiming to me, "You are humble, therefore you will be simultaneously in both realities at the party."

As the channeling continues, a healing commending Jeannie commences. The Holy Spirit surrounds her in a golden aura of spinning, psychedelic colors pronouncing, "You are blessed," and she becomes a young girl. Mother Mary puts her arms around Jeannie and kisses her on the cheek. We both thank Linda for this intersession.

Describing the tent, tables, balloons, food, and drinks that I order, Jeannie contends, "Sunday will be the only clear, sunny day of the week." (It pours on Friday when they set up the tent. It rains most of Saturday, all day Monday, and Tuesday.)

♥♥♥

Finally on Sunday morning the weather is beautiful. I rise early and set the tables with graduation banners and balloons. Since the color theme as Susan indicates in the invitation is yellow, mostly everyone complies with her request by wearing yellow. I bring out several collages of Linda, placing them on a table with flowers to honor the graduate.

When I finish setting everything up, I break down sobbing, yearning for her presence, "A graduation party without the graduate!" After a good cry, Linda speaks, "Now you feel better, let's have a blast!"

Over 60 friends and relatives celebrate Linda's graduation from the Earth Life System. I write a speech and Linda channels a speech through my higher self:

*"Today we celebrate a graduation from the Earth Life School, a graduation which we all will rejoice in when we complete our own journey.*

*"What is the Earth Life School or Earth Life System? It is a series of incarnations the soul, the spiritual or higher self makes lifetime after lifetime in order to work through its lessons of love, ego, judgment, passion, disappointment, merriment, jealousy, caring, giving, appreciation of goodness and beauty, attachments to material goods and wants, selfishness, insights, and relationships with itself and*

*others. Summed up in a single word, karma.*

*"When these lessons are learned, the soul is truly absolved of trials and tests, achieving victory and triumph over the human condition. It releases from the Earth Life System and graduates, unhindered to pursue other realms as other forms, until it becomes one with all that is.*

*"Sobering as it sounds, including all its wonders, majesty, and beauty, this incarnation is the lowest vibrational composition. But, we all have to start somewhere and this is a good place to begin our development.*

*"Linda asks to say a few words and I have written them down:*

*"I thank you all for coming on this special day, this distinctive event. It is very rare in the physical that you are able to share in something which is so exciting to us on the other side.*

*"But this graduation is not just for me, it is for all of you, too. By being here, you are witnesses to the power of unconditional love, the one true reason for your existence on this or any other plane.*

*"The drama of the personality is an illusion; it is not authentic. Only pureness within your hearts is what causes you to ascend in the light. We all get there because God is all good and cherishes us all. We hurt ourselves when we live with bitterness and negativity, realizing the pain and suffering we have caused ourselves and others.*

*"Forgive each other. Hold no jealousies, animosities, or opinions of each other, for these slow our elevation in the light. But when we clear these energies, we rejoice in the fulfilling bliss of undeniable blessedness and euphoria; the wondrous colors, the creation of enchanted premises we can inhabit on the other side to share with our loved ones, tasting, smelling, visualizing, and touching.*

*"So believe in our presence at the dinner table, a sunset, a party, when driving alone in a car, or listening to a song.*

*"I want to thank Annie for the beautiful collage she made of my time here and for adopting Nash [Annie's new puppy]. Susan brings all of you here today; the other side bowing to her in homage. My father, through his work on my side and on your side with his friends Karen, Harriette, and especially Jeannie, the medium blessed with the facility of healing, all channel and empower me to finish my work. These people and my consecrated guides have been the instruments to my freedom in the light.*

*"I bring blessings to all. Many loved ones in our lives have come to share this juncture. All you have to do is think of them right now and throughout the day because they are here amongst you. By doing this, you help them ascend and they in turn become empowered to help you on your earthen voyage.*

*"So shed a tear of jubilation and exhilaration, not remorse or sadness. Let the ecstasy of this moment fill your lives forever. Enjoy here. Lift the veil and permit us to share in your life."*

I then play the song "Little Star," by Madonna. Susan picks the song acknowledging Linda is a huge Madonna fan. Some of the lyrics capturing this day:

Never forget who you are

Little star

My life, my soul

You make my spirit whole

Shining brighter than all the stars in the sky

Never forget how to dream

Butterfly

Never forget where you come from

From love

You are a treasure to me

You are my star

May the angels protect you

May goodness surround you

My love I have found you


. . . DURING THE SONG, I AM DRAWN INTO AN OBE, ARRIVING AT LINDA'S CONFIRMATION PARTY ON A WARM OCTOBER AFTERNOON. SHE IS WEARING A SILVER DRESS WITH MATCHING SHOES, SMILING, SHOWING OFF HER NEW BRACES STRAIGHT FROM MY OFFICE. THERE ARE 120 RELATIVES AND FRIENDS DRINKING; LAUGHING; EATING LASAGNA, MEATBALLS, FRIED CALAMARI, EGGPLANT PARMIGIANA, CHICKEN ROLLATINI, BAKED CLAMS, ZUPPA DI MUSSELS, VEAL SCALLOPINI, PENNE ALLA VODKA, SALAD, AND HOMEMADE ITALIAN BREAD.

A CONGA LINE FORMS AND EVERYONE JOINS IN WHILE THE DJ ANNOUNCES THAT LINDA WANTS TO SING A SONG. SHE TAKES THE MICROPHONE SINGING AND DANCING TO "LIKE A PRAYER" BY MADONNA, AS IF LINDA AND I ARE ALONE IN MY DEN:


LIFE IS A MYSTERY

EVERYONE MUST STAND ALONE

I HEAR YOU CALL MY NAME

AND IT FEELS LIKE HOME

I HEAR YOUR VOICE

IT'S LIKE AN ANGEL SIGHING

I HAVE NO CHOICE, I HEAR YOUR VOICE

FEELS LIKE FLYING

IT'S LIKE A DREAM

NO END AND NO BEGINNING

YOU'RE HERE WITH ME

LET THE CHOIR SING

THE CROWD IS ON THEIR FEET, ELECTRIFIED, SHOUTING, CHEERING, MOVING WITH LINDA AND I AM SPEECHLESS. SHE IS THE PARTY . . .

At the conclusion of "Little Star," I continue speaking to the guests:

*"In closing, Linda constantly accompanies me. We have a Tiffany lamp on the piano, with two 100-watt bulbs activated by a pull chain. Friday night I shut the lamp on my way up to bed. Annie comes home well after midnight. If those lights are on, she would notice them shining brightly at the base of the stairs. Susan doesn't turns the lamp on or off. It is something I do every day. When I descend the steps for breakfast Saturday morning the lamp is off. After breakfast, as I walk back upstairs, both lights are on!*

*"It is now time to release the butterflies, the symbol of independence, of metamorphosis from frail humanity to divineness. As these butterflies rise up, remember we live forever. So if you expect to die one day, you may be disappointed."*

The butterflies fly out of their envelopes, Monarchs and Painted Ladies, more than 150 in all. Linda appears as a little girl, chasing butterflies alongside my ten-year-old cousin Sal and the rest of the children at the party. I wear a yellow shirt with pink, red, purple, and yellow butterflies shaped as a heart over my actual one. One of the Painted Ladies lands on the center of my heart amazing all the guests.

You can view the video of the *Butterfly Release at Linda La Batto's ELS Graduation* on YouTube. (In ten years people will ask, "What is YouTube?") It is a little more than three minutes long. Keep the volume low because my three-year-old twin girl cousins pick this moment to act up and I see Linda laughing. Kids will be kids.

Linda fancies balloons and asks me to release them in the sky to honor all on the other side who attend the party.

*Linda with balloons at age six*

My nephew Nick sings and my nephew Joseph plays the ukulele to one of Linda and my sister Terry's favorite songs, "Somewhere Over the Rainbow" from their favorite movie together. This video, *Linda La Batto-Somewhere Over the Rainbow,* is also on YouTube.

Linda and Terry always watch *The Wizard of Oz* together. Terry does the voices of the Wicked Witch, Glinda, Auntie Em, Dorothy, and the Scarecrow; Linda, the Tin Man and Toto. My father chimes in as the Cowardly Lion and I portray the voice of The Wizard. This is the reason why she channels the Yellow Brick Road.

*Linda with her paternal grandfather Nick and Aunt Terry*

# The Bank

Here is an indisputable example of Linda alive on the other side. Beginning with a little succinct background, I purchased a condo on Sanibel Island at the height of the real estate and banking boom in 2006. Recognizing the initials succeeding my name, the bank issued me a ten-year interest-only mortgage. The bank shall remain nameless because some very good people helped me along the way; all a matter of public record. So when everything fell apart in 2008, I, accompanied by millions of other people, was left with unmanageable debt and loss of income.

In July 2010 a written report resulting from an interview with HUD stated I was in a negative cash flow and my property was "underwater." I presented this documentation to the bank, asking for a modification, being furnished with a forbearance instead. I signed the agreement on November 30th until a study of all my financial records could be made; calling the bank every month, allocating monthly electronic transfers of funds to pay the forbearance, keeping dates and confirmation numbers, and always speaking to the same representative. During this period, I hired an attorney from Ft. Myers, Florida, to handle my case.

Finally, in August 2012, I received a letter stating my modification was denied. Calling my friend John, a Volvo salesman, I asked him to run a credit check on me.

He informed me, "The bank reported you haven't paid your mortgage in almost two years and your FICO credit score is 630." I spoke to my attorney about this and sent him over all the information. My go-to person at the bank knew Linda and liked her. When I told her of this, she gave me the phone number of the Senior Vice President of the Retention Division. When I called him, he petulantly asked, "How did you get my number?" After my attorney sent him all of the documentation, I received an e-mail response from the Senior Vice President stating there was nothing he could or would do and my credit report would remain as is.

In a session with Jeannie on November 10th, I ask Linda for help. She conveys to me, "Dad, look at the bank papers, there you will find mistakes. The bank intimidates everyone; paperwork, fine print, the illusion they are always right. I put a white dome around your attorney; he will help you and you shall prevail."

That evening I thumbed through every paper I ever received from the bank. After many hours, I finally uncovered two major mistakes. One was the bank's failure to inform me in writing of the sale of my mortgage to another lender within the first 30 days. (The mortgage was sold the day after my closing.) The second was that the forbearance agreement stated there would be no negative credit reporting during the forbearance period.

I e-mailed these pages to my attorney who forwarded them, along with a letter, to the Senior Vice President who once again stated nothing would be done and foreclosure proceedings would now be initiated.

I meet with Jeannie on February 27th, 2013. In this session Linda retorts, "The bank is shuffling papers all over in a fluster of confusion and I see you signing over the condo to a new owner. Everything will be over by the end of this spring and your credit report will be corrected." Two days later, on March 1st, the bank sends me an official letter stating they will authorize a short sale.

When I called my real estate agent, Judy Reddington, telling her of this, she reiterated, "Frank, I haven't received anything from the bank. They have to assign a contact person to handle the loan to appraise the property. Then I have to list it at their appraised value and we have to send offers from perspective buyers to the bank. It takes months to accept a buyer, and, from the signing of the contract to closing is at least an additional six to eight months."

On April 6th, seven years to the date I closed on the condo, the bank accepted an offer from a buyer and we all signed the contract. Three weeks later, an approval letter by certified mail stated the closing must be no later than June 21st, and the bank shall report any debt forgiveness to the IRS and I shall be responsible for $0 deficiency.

I was contacted by a bank employee who admitted the bank had made an error in my credit reporting. "All negative credit shall be reversed in 60 days and your impeccable record restored. You are a valued customer and we want to do everything possible to keep you as such."

The short sale closed on June 20th, the last day of spring, as Linda said it would. Summer officially began on the East Coast of North America at 1:04 AM EST on June 21st. When the funds were dispersed, I was given a relocation check by the bank. On August 25th, after checking my credit report, I found everything was clean and my FICO score was 762.

You have to really adore Linda. Some box of gold coins on the Yellow Brick Road! Wouldn't you agree?

# Summer 2013

The summer of 2013 held many surprises, the first of which occurred on Friday, June 21st. Susan is a letter carrier. While waiting at a red light in her small mail truck, a car sped around the corner, hit the car in front of Susan's truck, and then hit Susan head-on in her vehicle. The mail trucks have no air bags. Susan was taken by ambulance to the emergency room at South Nassau Communities Hospital in Oceanside, Long Island. I followed behind in my car.

Keep in mind that my communication and interaction with Linda or anyone else on the other side is always in the now, in the present, as I mention earlier. To be repetitive, so as not to confuse anyone, all things happen simultaneously due to no time or space on the other side.

In the emergency room, I witness the work of angels and healers, better than any episode of *ER* or *Grey's Anatomy*. Guardian angels holding the hands of patients, helping them; angels as healing guides hovering over the doctors, assisting and communicating with the physicians through their Crown Chakras, who then instruct the nurses to perform the exact tests and procedures on the patients as relayed through the angels and healers.

Susan's dad is standing by her bed, holding her hand. Linda is by my side relating, "You are able to see all this because you exist in both realities. This is why you are here, so others will believe all is continuous."

In a session with Jeannie the subsequent day, she informs me, "Linda consoles you the morning of the Graduation Party while you are crying heavily. All the celestials are jubilant as they share in the physical celebration of Linda's graduation from The Earth Life System." Jeannie also confirms Linda is next to me in the hospital last night.

Linda then announces, "A visitor wants to talk to you." An apparition alights in the room and converses with me. This figure appears thrice over the summer, revealing things to me, finally making Someone known to me before summer's end.

I say to Jeannie, "Susan and I are going to Europe at the end of September. We want Linda on our trip. It's her graduation present." Linda answers, "I shall be with you for the entire time. A soul always travels amidst a loved one, especially if that soul is a child who transitions. I am part of you, in you, and with you forever."

On Thursday, June 27th, I connect my iPhone to the car's Bluetooth and play my greatest hits shuffle. It contains over 1800 songs, none of which are doubles. "I Got You Babe" plays five times in a row and I weep as Linda comments, "The words in this song are important. Listen. It defines us!"

And when I'm sad, you're a clown
And if I get scared, you're always around–
Then put your little hand in mine
There ain't no hill or mountain
We can't climb–
I got you to hold my hand
I got you to understand

I got you to walk with me
I got you to talk with me
I got you to kiss goodnight
I got you to hold me tight
I got you, I won't let go
I got you to love me so
I got you babe

At 10:00 PM on July 14th, I shut all the lights on the third floor of my home, but, at 2:00 AM the lights are back on; the glass-paned door to the third floor is still closed as I left it the previous evening. When I ascend the steps, three 60-watt bulbs are burning brightly on the ceiling fan. There are no switches on the second floor for the third floor, you must go upstairs and physically turn them on.

Monday evening, July 29th, as I am writing at my desk, Linda's 8x10 wooden-framed Communion picture, 15 feet away, topples off the bookshelf and onto the carpet. The bookshelf is built solidly into the wall and there are no tremors in the house the moment the picture falls. All the other pictures remain intact.

*Linda's First Communion Photo*

How about some frivolity and spontaneity? The first weekend in August, my cousin Samantha has a bachelorette getaway on Fire Island. Simultaneously, with Susan feeling a little better, we venture to Shorecrest Bed and Breakfast on the North Fork of Long Island.

On Friday we wind up at Lieb Cellars, a winery in Cutchogue. As we sit outside contemplating the beautiful field of yellow flowers while tasting wine, an adult Linda sits next to us. She sips wine, grinning, as Susan and I are telling funny stories. Later that evening at The Sound View Restaurant in Greenport, we secure a table overlooking the beach. As dinner is being served, Linda occupies the empty seat at our table watching the sun set.

Saturday morning around 2:00 AM, with beach chairs facing the ocean on Fire Island, my cousins Angela, Jessica, and Samantha, with their friends Elaine, Lauren, and Lindsay start talking about Linda. Lindsay, who has psychic abilities, never meets Linda but perceives her presence often. As they are experiencing Linda's company, facing a calm ocean, a single huge wave breaks onto the shore. The water forcefully rushes 30 feet up the sand, stopping at the base of their chairs. Afterward, the ocean immediately returns to placidity.

. . . AT 6:00 AM, I ROLL OUT OF MY BODY. LINDA IS HOLDING MY HAND IN BED, SMILING, SAYING, "LET'S GO OUTSIDE AND SIT IN THE GARDEN." SHE IS SEVEN OR EIGHT YEARS OLD. WE BOTH GET UP, WALK OUTSIDE, AND ROCK IN THE HAMMOCK IN FRONT OF THE BEAUTIFUL ENGLISH GARDENS THAT SURROUND THE PROPERTY OF THE BED AND BREAKFAST. WE WATCH THE MAGNIFICENT SUNRISE ILLUMINATING THE KALEIDOSCOPE OF COLORFUL FLORAL DISPLAYS. THE PERFUME OF ORCHARDS OVERWHELMS MY SENSES; BLUE JAYS, CARDINALS, ROBINS, SPARROWS, WHITE DOVES, AND HUMMINGBIRDS DANCE AMONG THE BUSHES. HONEYBEES BUZZ AS THEY PERFORM THEIR EARLY MORNING RITUALS WHILE BUTTERFLIES OF ALL SIZES, SHAPES, AND COLORS POLLINATE THE WILD ANNUALS AND PERENNIALS. RABBITS, CHIPMUNKS, POSSUMS, AND FIELD MICE DART IN AND OUT OF THE

UNDERBRUSH.

As we rock back and forth, my right arm around Linda's shoulder, I softly kiss her cheek twice. She hugs me; her touch and warmth are as clear as this splendid summer's morn. I am overcome with the absoluteness of her manifestation. Then she gets up and walks into the beautiful English gardens . . .

On Tuesday of the following week, August 6th, Susan calls me at work. She says, "I am vacuuming the hardwood steps leading up to the second floor. When I get to the step even with the top of the piano, the one which is even with Linda's pictures, vase, and urn, the high hats on the ceiling over the piano turn on." The only switch is on the wall at the foyer entrance, some 25 feet away.

On September 6th, Susan and I attend the wedding of my cousins Kevin and Samantha at Land's End on the inlet in Sayville, New York. This is my first wedding since Linda's transition, one which she would have physically attended. I do not have any alcohol this evening, wanting to be totally aware of Linda's presence, embracing what is necessary for my healing and growth.

In honor of Linda, they play "Like a Prayer" and she dances in a gold dress along with other celestials who attend. I share private moments with Linda by the water's edge.

But my greatest challenge is when my cousin Scott dances with his daughter Samantha, something I will never experience in this reality. Courageously, I stand and watch, my arm around Susan's waist, extremely exuberant for Scott who has just beaten non-Hodgkin's lymphoma and is able to dance with his daughter at her wedding.

Permitting my humanity and wounds to be present, Linda consoles me. "You will be fine," she annunciates, and with that my cousin John places his hand on my shoulder to comfort me. Born six months apart, we are raised like brothers, our mothers were and still are sisters. I shall be forever grateful for his compassion and tenderness at this moment.

The next day, I meet with Jeannie, who asserts, "Linda is at the wedding wearing a gold dress. She dances with you, understanding your confusion and turmoil. There are many celestials and guides to comfort you."

# A Messenger Angel and
# The King of Kings

In a session with Jeannie on June 22nd, an angelic being with wings appears, a super soul, a female, and Linda enunciates, "Dad, you must come out of your body, going very deep, to communicate with this divineness." . . . In an OBE I am brought to a location I have been to previously, melding with this intelligence in a realm of all knowing and rapture.

She declares, "Linda and I are here guiding you, granting your wishes, helping you to complete your mission of writing the book. You have extreme humility given the responsibilities that are bestowed upon you. Other heavenly beings, including Linda, are here to support you."

Taken to the top of a mountain, my arms outstretched, this eternal asks what I want. I answer, "To enable mankind to awaken, to lift the veil, to truly envelop the all-encompassing. Humanity must move beyond the animal drive that has led us to revel in darkness thousands of years in the Earth Life System."

She replies, "Considering what you ask is pure selflessness, you are acknowledged and heard." I then join with Linda in a rhapsody of

Re-entering my body, I comment to Jeannie, "It is so hard to come back and stay on this plane after being totally immersed on the other side." During this session, Jeannie witnesses my anatomy vibrating; colors pouring forth from my Chakra points.

In a session with Jeannie on July 31st, both Linda and the Holy Spirit come to me. The Holy Spirit professes, "You and Linda are twin entities and will travel as equal companions. A point will come where you will have to choose between two directions, both guided in the light. Whichever course you choose, Linda is truly happy and won't be effected."

On August 16th, the Holy Spirit again appears in the suite with Jeannie and me. Linda expounds, "The Holy Spirit wants to show you a page in the Book of Life," and opens the book. I am shown a beautiful waterfall, flowers of yellow and white lining the rocks along its sides, grass and trees glowing with diamond-like intensity, and the words *Peace* and *God*; three white doves are flying over my head, the Trinity upon me.

The Holy Spirit enunciates, "The doves signify your answering life's experiences and your eventual transfiguration into completeness. Write the book working with those who have been sent to you."

Viewing another page, I discern all of my family and friends on both sides receiving the same healing, playing as joyful young children. I ask the Holy Spirit if my current odyssey is in the Book of Life. "But a page" is the reply.

On August 24th, Linda asserts with Jeannie present, "The significant incarnate is amongst us once more, the glorified one with the golden hair. You are to travel on the wings of this super soul." . . . LEAVING MY BODY IN AN OBE I TRAVEL ON ONE WING, LINDA ON THE OTHER. WE ARE SHOWN ESPLANADES FILLED WITH BEAUTY, PEACE, AND MAGNIFICENT COLORS.

STANDING ON A CLIFF, I VIEW A VILLAGE OF STONE ON MY LEFT, THE SEA BELOW TO MY RIGHT, THE STARS AND MOON SHINING BRIGHTLY; A GENTLE WIND GUIDING THE SEA ONTO THE SHORE. LINDA IS MY GIFT, MY TEACHER, AND I HONOR HER COURAGE. LIGHTNING SHOOTS OUT FROM MY RIGHT FOOT.

ASKING AGAIN WHAT I WANT, I REPLY, "INNER PEACE AND FREEDOM TO BRING ALL THE BEAUTY OF CREATION WITH ME WHEN I TRANSITION; FAVORING OTHERS TO EXPERIENCE THESE THINGS SERVING SIMULTANEOUSLY ON BOTH PLANES." A BLESSING IS BESTOWED OVER *LINDA IN THE LIGHT* AND I HEAR ANGELS SINGING "GLORIA IN EXCELSIS DEO." "IT IS DONE" THE ETERNAL CONFIRMS . . .

Still in expansive awareness upon re-joining the physical, I channel for Jeannie, saying, "Here are a dozen roses, a crown, and a golden cape. You allow these events to occur by creating a space of unrestricted limitless sacredness. With your faith in God, Jeannie, you too can fly on the wings of the angelic soul."

It is finally revealed to me in a session with Jeannie and Linda on September 14th, the messenger angel, the super soul, the one who appears to me twice before asking questions, is preparing me for this day.

During this session with Linda and the super soul guardian present, I am taken into a profound meditation revealing God the Father, the Holy Spirit, and Mother Mary. Colors vibrate in front of my eyes. This meeting takes place on the other side and at this point Linda gives me the greatest of gifts!

Jeannie exclaims, "This is the most powerful session I have ever experienced!" Surrounded in a white fluorescence I am taken to a pilgrimage during biblical times. Linda is with me on this expedition. I bow in humility, kissing the feet of Linda and all of my lifetimes. I accept true compassion for myself and all the souls, including Linda, who are my teachers and who make sacrifices so Linda and I can fulfill our destiny; forgiving all injustices inflicted upon me and am forgiven for injustices I conferred upon others.

Jesus immediately unveils Himself and Jeannie professes, "Jesus never reveals Himself until you are ready for His intervention." I am filled with understanding and the acknowledgment of God and man as One.

Jesus commands, "Lazarus, come forth!" I then comprehend the miracle, the significance, the symbolism of Lazarus. I witness Christ, lifting the shroud between physical and non-physical existence, authorizing Lazarus' spirit to re-inhabit his body after leaving this earthly plane some four days prior, shattering the illusion of the finality of death for human beings by breathing life into someone just like you and me. Yet we remain clouded in judgment, blocking this benefaction when we lose a loved one, especially a child, a teacher, someone like Jesus, who sacrifices for us.

The transition of a child is a fulfillment of a pre-ordained agreement. We recognize and acknowledge the miracle of God resurrecting his Son so we will know of our immortality. This is our birthright, something unquestionable and supreme, yet we sometimes question this when our children ascend to life everlasting.

Jesus continues, "I send the deistic who manifests to you. Now you are ready to see me because you desire exoneration for all on all levels, releasing the betrayal, the Judas in yourself and in all men. Yes, he sits beside me for he represents the love and forgiveness God has regarding all of His children. My Father is all good, all loving, creating out of pure glory, joy, and Divine perfection. He raises all to Him as they fulfill the promises they make to Him before entering the anatomical."

When the session ends, I think a little over a minute has passed. Jeannie remarks, "You have been in the splendor of grace one and one half hours." I thank Linda, supporting her choices, her courage, and her generosity to me on this special day.

# Europe 2013

Finally it's time for our vacation to Europe to rejoice and be festive. As stated previously, my interactions with Linda or any celestial being is always in the now due to no chronology (time) or substantive structure (space) on the other side. This natural way of communicating, this essential birthright available to all, is something we experience with those not of physicality. Consequently, most of what I write is in the present.

Susan is in a lot of discomfort from the accident, so she is fitted with a neck and back brace for the trip. On Friday, September 27th, prior to boarding the flight from JFK in New York to Charles de Gaulle in Paris, Linda announces, "Susan will not be in pain the entire trip and we are going to have a good time." True to her word, Susan only feels stiffness and aches throughout our travels!

As we board the full plane, there is only one unoccupied seat, the window recliner adjacent to Susan. This *empty seat* phenomenon occurs at every restaurant, whether lunch or dinner (breakfast is usually staggered at the hotels with plenty of seats available), during our ten-day tour; on every excursion, Eurostar train ride from Paris to London, and our flight home from Heathrow to JFK.

Everyone who travels to Europe knows seating is at a premium in cafés and restaurants. Often strangers will sit at your table, initiate conversation, and eat next to you.

Linda accompanies us as an adult throughout Europe, being jovial, making her individuality apparent. When we arrive at the Napoleon Hotel on Avenue de Friedland, we are given an upgraded suite with a spare room for Linda. When I position my iPod in the iPod clock radio, "I Got You Babe" plays, and I start to cry: Linda is here!

Throughout our stay at the Napoleon, Linda constantly changes the time on that clock radio. Good thing I have the front desk wake us up each morning.

Lunch is across from our hotel at Le Café de Paris, where we sit outside in the glass-enclosed veranda and people-watch; the space adjoining us remaining empty for Linda. Lunch behind us, we take a leisurely stroll down the Champs-Élysées, Susan holding my left hand, Linda my right.

That evening we find ourselves at Casa Luca on Avenue Marceau, celebrating Susan's birthday. The restaurant is packed, with only one place setting available with Linda sitting there singing "Happy Birthday" to Susan along with myself and the wait staff. She helps Susan blow out the candles. As we meander back to our hotel, Susan buys a pack of French cigarettes and smokes one and I laugh because Linda is smoking a cigarette too!

On Sunday, our driver Julian takes Susan, Linda, and me around Paris. We light candles at Notre-Dame Cathedral, walk through the Montmartre section and watch the artists paint outside in front of the quaint cafés. "You enjoy this," Linda remarks, "You should paint outdoors, too."

We lunch at Café Kléber, at Place du Trocadéro; once again only one unoccupied seat for Linda. We take an afternoon tour of the Eiffel Tower. At the second level observation deck, Linda pronounces, "Dad, I am at the wedding and you are forever generous. When we are back home, send Kevin and Samantha an additional gift to acknowledge my attending." (Before the wedding, I am troubled by the anguish of Linda not being there anatomically and uncertain as to how much money I should give. Linda understands this and wants me to show the joyous appreciation of her appearance.)

I become anxious as we ride to the top of the tower in an elevator not visualizing what to expect, so Linda comments, "It's okay at the top, you'll see. Everything is enclosed and you will fancy the beauty of Paris." When the elevator doors part, I am delighted for Linda is correct.

Dinner is at Le Deauville on the Champs-Élysées. The restaurant is very crowded with no extra placings available, except one honoring Linda. She inhabits my body as I try lamb, beef, pork, duck and several different wines. "Thank you for inviting me on this trip, allowing me to taste the food and savor the wines," she utters.

On Monday, Susan's and my second wedding anniversary, the three of us take a beautiful saunter down the Champs-Élysées to the Louvre. We stop along the way at Les Jardin des Tuileries to admire the beautiful landscape, snacking on hot buns. Susan sits down on a bench and drinks a cup of coffee with Linda adjacent to her smoking a cigarette. Paris is Linda's kind of city.

Lunch takes place at Le Royal on Rue la Fayette, a very busy establishment amid a lot of businessmen and women packed almost on top of one another. Waiting 15 minutes, we are accommodated at a table with only one vacancy next to me in the whole restaurant for you know who! At the Louvre, Linda apprises the artwork and statues, including the *Mona Lisa*.

Susan and I book a dinner cruise on the River Seine, securing a cozy table for two up front; an extra chair positioned next to me. We just laugh and don't ask why. Linda stands out on the deck beside me as I take photos of Paris at night. When we get back to our hotel, it is such a delightful evening we decide to rest outside and take pleasure in the nighttime air, enjoying a cup of coffee. Linda encompasses me, transferring her complete joy and excitement, allowing me to envision one of her past lives living in Paris and working in a hotel.

On Tuesday we do a little shopping along the Champs-Élysées and lunch in our room. After lunch, we board a small mini-van, an unattended seat for Linda, anticipating a tour of the Palace of Versailles. She is entertained during the tour of the palace and the enchanted gardens, showing me the illusions of the kings, "All favoring ego, nothing is valid."

We eat dinner at Villa d'Este on Rue Arsène Houssaye, which is in walking distance from the Napoleon. Affixing herself in the only unoccupied place setting in the restaurant, Linda chuckles as we make conversation during dinner. As we return to the hotel, Susan lights up one of her cigarettes and Linda does the same.

The following day, we all walk to the Arc de Triomphe, taking the elevator to the top. It is a clear morning in Paris and the view breathtaking. Linda observes, "This is a magnificent view of the city."

Susan and I sit lunching once again at Le Café de Paris, the usual empty spot open to my right; awaiting the mini-van that will take us to Giverny, Monet's Gardens, and the Normandy countryside. We have the same tour guide from yesterday, four of us physically in attendance and one non-physically. Guess who? We stop at the church where Claude Monet and his family are laid to rest. As the others walk up the hill, I remain behind at the gravesite.

Linda articulates, "Dad, I brought the tour guide here because Claude Monet wants to meet you." He steps forward and declares, "Thank you for staying behind to talk to me, honoring my family's memory. This is Linda's surprise for you, showing you her gratitude for coming on this trip." (Linda knows I have three Monet prints in my home and one in my office. I take pleasure painting in oils.)

. . . I AM USHERED BY CLAUDE MONET IN AN OBE, BACK TO LINDA'S APARTMENT

ON STATEN ISLAND. I HAVE MY CAMERA WITH ME, ABOUT TO LAUNCH A PHOTO SHOOT OF LINDA FOR AN OIL PORTRAIT. SHE IS IN THE BEDROOM PUTTING ON MAKEUP WHILE I AM BEING ENTERTAINED BY HER FOUR CATS AND TWO YORKIES. EMERGING FROM THE BEDROOM, THRILLED, SHE PROCLAIMS, "I'M READY." TAKING DIFFERENT PHOTOS OF LINDA; STRAIGHT ON, HEAD TILTED UP, TILTED DOWN, SMILING, SERIOUS, ¼ TURN TO THE LEFT, THEN THE RIGHT, FULL PROFILE LEFT, FULL PROFILE RIGHT; SOME DELIBERATION ENSUES AND WE BOTH AGREE ON HER RIGHT SIDE PROFILE.

I SURPRISE HER WITH THE PAINTING ON HER 22ND BIRTHDAY, FRAME AND ALL, CAPTURING THE QUINTESSENTIAL LINDA, THE PERSONIFICATION OF HER INDIVIDUALITY, TIMELESS, UNFALTERING. IT IS MY LABOR OF ADMIRATION TO MY FOREVER SWEETHEART . . .

*My oil portrait of Linda, 2007*

When we reach Monet's Gardens, I really have to use the restroom. The tour guide informs me it is in the gift shop at the far end of the gardens, past Monet's house. Many people like myself take a high blood pressure pill with a diuretic and when the diuretic kicks in, your urge to relieve yourself is uncontrollable. Monet utters, "You won't need to use the bathroom because Linda shall help you. Enjoy yourself."

Walking through the garden with Linda, Susan takes photos where Monet painted the pictures that are in our house. A beautiful, colorful butterfly lands on a pink carnation in front of us. We tour Monet's home and finally two hours later we reach the gift shop. As I happen to glance up reading a sign pointing to the men's room I say, "Wow, Linda controls my bodily functions from the other side." Leisurely I enter the rest room.

On our way back to the hotel, driving through the Normandy countryside, we pass a large castle. Linda whispers, "This is where Rommel stays while Germany occupies France." When I mention this to our tour guide, she replies, "Not many people have this information. How did you get it?" I nonchalantly interject, "Oh, I have a hunch."

Our last night in Paris, we dine at L'Etoile 1903, on Avenue de Wagram. The food is excellent; Linda once again at a chair in a crowded restaurant where no other empty settings are to be found. She asks to taste the food; the familiar shift materializes, happening so often I am lost when Linda doesn't intermingle.

Thursday we board the train from Paris Nord station to St. Pancras in London. Linda waits with me in the dining car as I order coffee and tea, stating, "Stare out the window and take in the captivating French countryside."

We arrive at Flemings Mayfair Hotel on Half Moon Street, upgrading to an apartment with separate accommodations for Linda.

That afternoon, promenading through Green Park towards Buckingham Palace, Linda, pointing out Yorkshire Terriers in the park exclaims, "I can live here, too!" I realize why we are on this trip. It is something Linda wanted to do on Earth and I fulfill this promise to her, so she can encounter through me the sights and sounds of Europe. This is my gift to her.

We have dinner in our apartment that evening. The steward prepares three settings on the serving table, asking "Is the other person here yet?" My response is "Yes she is." Linda verbalizes to me, "I dig this apartment."

On Friday we have a private five-and-a-half-hour tour of London with our driver and guide, Lovett, a former BBC television producer who lives on actor Michael Caine's street. Linda and Susan are enjoying all the British movie and television stories Lovett shares with us throughout the drive. Linda has her contagious laugh, and is most pleased when we get out of the car, making several passes across Abbey Road, mimicking the Beatles' album cover.

Arriving back at our hotel, enjoying high tea at 4:00 PM, Linda convenes in the uninhabited place setting at our table with poise and grace, giggling, as Susan and I, having missed lunch, eat a little hastily.

That evening we amble to Le Boudin Blanc on Trebeck Street in Shepherd Market, a series of narrow winding streets containing many pubs and restaurants; a crowded, quaint area reminiscent of the back streets in Florence, Italy, and Greenwich Village in Manhattan.

We secure a table where the usual unfilled seat is there paying tribute to Linda. After dinner, as a kind gesture, the maître d' buys me a Drambuie while I sit outside smoking a Cuban cigar, joined by Linda and Susan who are smoking cigarettes, sipping red wine.

Saturday, October 5th, we witness the Changing of the Guard at Buckingham Palace. With tips from Lovett and Linda's guidance, we stand at the correct positions, seeing everything unobstructed from the large crowd. What an outstanding experience!

From Buckingham Palace, we hike to Harrods Department Store, eating lunch outdoors at Harrods Terrace. Linda takes in the rare October London sunshine, sitting on the only unoccupied stool. She tastes my coq au vin and accompanies us as we shop in the store.

Dinner is at Da Corradi, an Italian restaurant in Shepherd Market. The place is jam-packed; it helps that I speak Italian. The owner squeezes us into a little table downstairs where–you guess it–one extra seat is waiting for Linda. Simply amazing!

Leaving no time for digestion, Susan trumpets, "Let's go pub crawling." Linda chimes in, "Yeah, let's go. It will be a lot of fun." We hit The Market Tavern at the beginning and end of the crawl. In between we stop at Kings Arms, Shepherds Tavern, where Linda wanders over to pet a black poodle, and The Old Express.

As Susan and I stumble back to the apartment, Linda shouts, "What a vacation!" I respond, "If it hadn't been for your benefaction on the Yellow Brick Road, we wouldn't be here today. I adore you considering everything you have done to make this trip possible."

The following morning, waking up without a hangover or upset stomach, Linda giggles, "We have a plane to catch and you need to enjoy the ride home." Boarding the flight from Heathrow Airport to JFK, aligning in twin recliners near the rear of the 747, I notice adjoining Susan an opening large enough to fit a small seat; Linda snuggles in making herself comfortable.

♥♥♥

The time spent with Linda on this vacation is very special because I am able to exist simultaneously in both realms and there is no separation between them. I experience true knowing, receptive to the lifting of the veil, living in the moment, acknowledging what happens here is a just part of a larger continuum.

I share this European trip seeing I am a regular person with no special talents or abilities, just someone with an open mind willing to learn. What happens to me, happens to all and I hope this revelation awakens your individual journey, your road to encountering undeniable events with your children or loved ones in the light.

# Some Wonderful Moments

In a session with Jeannie on October 13th, she tells me of Linda living in Paris and London and she sees Linda smoking cigarettes with Susan during our vacation. "Linda is forever grateful considering the endless lovingness you share with her in Europe. She wants to watch movies with you this week." Blue beams emanate from me, I cannot move, and a OBE ensues . . .

. . . I AM OUT OF MY BODY. THE LIGHTS IN MY BEDROOM ARE OFF. AFTER WATCHING *HOOK*, LINDA RUNS IN WITH HER GLOWING PETER PAN SWORD AND I HAVE TO FEND HER OFF USING MY FAKE PLASTIC HAND WITH A HOOK ON IT. "I AM HERE TO SAVE THE LOST BOYS," SHE CRIES OUT. WE DO BATTLE ON MY BED UNTIL ONE OF US FALLS OFF, USUALLY ME, BECAUSE GETTING THE BIGGEST REACTION FROM HER IS ALL I WANT.

AFTER DETHRONING ME SEVEN OR EIGHT ENCOUNTERS, SHE BOLTS INTO HER BEDROOM AND RUNS OUT DONNING HER TEAM BASEBALL HAT AND GLOVE RETORTING, "HOW ABOUT WE WATCH *A LEAGUE OF THEIR OWN* NOW?" I AGREE FOR THE TENTH TIME IN THE PAST THREE WEEKS AS SHE SNUGGLES CLOSE ON THE RECLINER, HER EYES GLUED TO THE SCREEN, MY EYES SELFISHLY GLUED TO AN ENCHANTED MOMENT, ASKING, "WHAT DID I DO TO DESERVE THIS CHILD?" . . .

December finds me on a trip to San Diego to watch the Giants lose to the

Chargers. One morning my friend Pete and I are riding bikes along the beach when I pass upon a vaguely familiar spot. Linda suggests, "Stop here." I stop riding and wonder why?

She continues, "I am very sick this day in San Diego but I don't tell you. When I can't walk any further from the agony, I ask, 'Can we stop and buy some tee shirts?' You are so elated, Pete takes a picture of us right here. When you go home you shall locate the picture of me smiling. I am with you and that alone stops my suffering."

Pete sees my eyes flood with emotion and allows me some space with Linda on the bike path.

*Linda and me in San Diego*

On December 22nd, Linda wants me to bring flowers from her vase on the piano to the cemetery, honoring my sister Terry. While I remain at Terry's headstone, Linda arrives at my right side, Terry at my left and we all hug.

Terry enunciates, "Thank you for all you do for my family, helping me in the everlasting." I answer, "It's the least I can do. You keep Linda gleeful in the light as in her earthbound reality when you were both on this side."

On Christmas Eve, Susan and I are invited to cousins Ritchie and Lori's house. As I rest on their couch anticipating dinner, Linda aligns opposite me on the recliner as her adult self and simultaneously next to me on the couch as a six-year-old girl.

. . . I EMBARK UPON AN OBE. IT IS 7:00 AM CHRISTMAS MORNING. LINDA ENTERS MY BEDROOM TO WAKE ME UP, SHAKING ME WITH ALL HER MIGHT. "DAD," SHE ASSERTS IN A VOICE WHOLLY ELECTRIFIED, "WAKE UP, WAKE UP, THERE ARE PRESENTS UNDER THE TREE!" I NOTICE THE EARLY MORNING SAND IN THE CORNERS OF HER EYES AS SHE DARTS DOWN THE STEPS TO THE DEN.

"LOOK, LOOK! A BRAND NEW SLED AND NEW ICE SKATES. HE DRANK HIS MILK AND ATE HIS COOKIES TOO! GOOD THING WE PUT THEM NEAR THE FIREPLACE SO HE WOULDN'T MISS THEM. CAN WE GO SKATING AFTER BREAKFAST? HE EVEN FILLED MY STOCKING AND WROTE ME A CARD."

DEAR LINDA,

I KNOW YOU HAVE BEEN A GOOD GIRL

XOXOXO

SANTA CLAUS

SHE HANDS ME A PRESENT. "I GOT THIS IN SCHOOL FOR YOU BECAUSE MY TEACHER SAID ONLY CHILDREN GET PRESENTS FROM SANTA." I UNWRAP THE PACKAGE. IT IS A WOODEN FRAMED POEM BY MELBA ALLRED:

**DAD**

STRENGTH AND WISDOM TO GUARD ME,

A WARM AND KINDLY SMILE,

FUN AND JOY AND LAUGHTER,

STRONG ARMS TO HUG ME AWHILE

FEARS, AND TEARS, AND TRIALS,

MANY KINDLY DEEDS,

FONDEST THOUGHTS AND MEMORIES

LOVE TO GUIDE AND LEAD.

**I LOVE YOU, LINDA**

CHRISTMAS PANCAKES COMPLETE, WE HEAD TO THE ICE SKATING RINK. I NEVER SAW ANYONE LACE UP SKATES SO FAST. SHE ALREADY DOES TWO COMPLETE REVOLUTIONS ROUND THE RINK BEFORE I CATCH UP WITH HER, GRABBING HER HAND. WITH ALL HER ENTHUSIASM, SHE BLURTS OUT, "DAD, I CAN SKATE BACKWARDS," TURNING, FACING ME AS SHE DOES THIS WONDROUS FEAT.

ONE OF OUR NEIGHBORS GOES PAST US. SIX-YEAR-OLD LINDA ARTICULATES VERY INTUITIVELY, "HE IS SAD SINCE HIS GRANDDAUGHTER DIED LAST MONTH."

WE FINISH SKATING AND I AM GLAD SINCE SHE IS SO HARD TO KEEP UP WITH. OUT OF BREATH I SAY, "LET'S GO TO AUNT TERRY'S AND DISCOVER MORE SURPRISES FROM SANTA."

"WHY DOES SANTA BRING TOYS ON CHRISTMAS?" SHE ASKS WITH ADORABLE INNOCENCE. "SANTA CLAUS DROPS PRESENTS OFF TO CHILDREN TODAY SHOWING HIS LOVE FOR THEM AND HE EVEN BRINGS SOME TO CHILDREN TOMORROW, HAVING SO MANY HE CAN'T FIT THEM ALL ON HIS SLEIGH IN ONE NIGHT." . . . but this gala OBE ends as Susan nudges me.

Towards the end of December, I'm back playing the piano, which always makes Linda very festive. Souls revere singing and music; the immaculate reverberation resonates in the glorious and the supreme. As I play "White Christmas," Linda acknowledges it by knocking over our Christmas picture on the piano while the other five photos remain upright undisturbed.

*The Christmas photo Linda knocks over*

January 2014 finds Susan and me on Sanibel Island vacationing. While riding bikes one sunny afternoon, Linda requests, "I want to savor the ocean breeze, the warmth of the sun, the smell of the orchards; to inhale the breath of your world again." I say, "Absolutely," as we become one. I am ebullient, grateful, honored, yet melancholy, missing her companionship, but elated beyond this embodiment.

While Susan is collecting shells on the beach, I sit beside Linda emoting tears of jubilation because I exist with her on two planes simultaneously.

On Saturday, February 15th, after one of the horrendous ice and snow storms that hit Long Island, I open my front door as my sister-in-law Lori is coming up the walkway. Our dog Nash, without his collar, darts out past me. Lunging with my slippers on to grab him, my feet hit the ice, my legs fly into the air; I am about to slide on my back down three slate steps and at least fracture my coccyx bone. Instantaneously, Nash and I stop as if an invisible wall prevents us from falling.

Linda calls out, "Do you really think I would tolerate your getting hurt."

One morning in March, while dressing, my father walks past me, his hands touching my back, saying, "Turn around. Someone wants to talk to you." I turn and see a 12-year-old Linda resting in my bed, her voice resonating in my ear, "You can stop crying now."

Working out in my gym on the third floor of our home on April 14th, I perceive little resistance from the weights. I stop exercising to check the setting and it registers 80 pounds. I return to my routine but it still feels like 20 pounds.

Linda taps my shoulder, "I am helping you work out. Now you can finish by yourself." With that, the full resistance of the 80 pounds return. I yell out, "Holy!!!"

# Linda's Second Birthday in the Light

On May 5th, waking up at 7:15 AM, I open the bedroom window and lie on the floor. Linda manifests next to me, "Remember, as a newborn home from the hospital, you feed me, change me and we sit by the window, listening to birds, watching the sun rise, the flowers blooming their new leaves. You talk and sing to me, rocking me until I fall back to sleep and I am very happy in your arms. You are a great father."

Overjoyed reliving the emanation of unquestionable devotion, not wanting to lose the absolute, boundless, tenderness of her sweetness, I do not move. This is an unforgettable start to a beautiful day with Linda in the light.

At 9:00 AM, Linda asks, "Dad, can I hold all the animals now?" (One of Linda's friends with a farm adopted Cookie, Christie, Cher, and Little Kitten after Linda's transition because Susan and I were renovating our home on Long Island. Selfless in action, yet painful and heart-wrenching, we felt it unfair to confine six animals. Two of Linda's four cats, Caesar and Cleo, being brother and sister and the first to be adopted by her, often left the other four and wandered on their own, so we chose to take them.)

We enter Annie's room where I pick up Nash and discern Linda interlacing in me holding him. After walking into Susan's office, we play with her two guinea pigs, Gnocchi and Tartufo. Then strolling to the screened-in porch where Cleo and Caesar join us, we pick them up; Linda hugging and kissing them. When we finish, she exclaims, "Thank you for this wonderful birthday present!"

Later that morning I drive with Linda to the shrine of Mother Mary at Saint Paul's Cathedral in Hempstead, lighting candles honoring Linda and all my relatives and friends who transition. I kneel in devotion to Mary for all she does concerning Linda and me. Mary declares with a blessing, "Thank you for coming and paying homage."

While I'm sitting in the pew in front of the shrine meditating, Linda states very, very clearly, "Write under the title of the book, *'The Incredible True Story That Will Change Your Life Forever'!*"

Suddenly I am taken to a domain of voluminous consecration and sacredness where angels are singing; a tremendous surge of fervency overtakes my core and I am in a high vibrational expansiveness, filled with the Holy Spirit.

In the afternoon, Linda and I visit Jeannie for a special birthday treat. Linda is five years old at her birthday party playing on a swing set with other children. She has a short, bobbed haircut; her hearty, contagious laugh is making everyone around her festive.

She asks, "Dad, do you want to go deeper into an OBE?" I enunciate, "Yes." . . .

MY SUPER SOUL THEN APPEARS, NO CURTAIN SEPARATES US. I AM TAKEN TO A HABITAT WHERE I AND OTHERS GO IN AN NDE AND DON'T WANT TO LEAVE. ONCE AGAIN THE HAND OF GOD REACHES OUT TO ME. LINDA ANNOUNCES, "I HAVE AN AWARD COMMENDING YOU; A BLANK CANVAS TO PAINT ON. WHAT DO YOU SEE?" THE FACE OF JESUS IS BROUGHT FORTH AND NEXT TO HIS FACE IS A SHROUD OF COLORS WITH WHITE AND YELLOW EDGES.

I REPLY, "MY CANVAS IS PEACEFUL, FILLED WITH WILDLIFE, A WARM BREEZE FLOWING FROM THE SEA, UNOBSTRUCTED AND BOUNTIFUL, AND I WILL CONSTANTLY CREATE ON IT." . . .

Returning from this voyage, Jeannie remarks, "Linda is as an adult as you write the book, but she writes through you." (Remember, I call Linda the ghostwriter of this book!) Jeannie starts crying, "Linda is having the happiest of birthdays."

Back at home, I play "Circle of Life" on the piano. Linda sits on my lap, causing me to weep. Even though we freely communicate with one another and meld in all realities, I deeply miss her substance. The words of this song exemplify the interweaving of our lifetimes:

> It's the leap of faith
> It's the band of hope
> 'till we find our place
> on the path unwinding
> in the circle
> the circle of life.

After playing "Happy Birthday," Linda and I spend the rest of the day in the hot tub together, reminiscing and rejoicing out loud.

*Linda's seventh birthday, 1992*

All throughout the day and evening, people are calling and texting to see how I am doing. I am very honest with my sentiments, emotions, and thoughts when others ask, responding straightforwardly to all, "I am having a spectacular day with Linda, the most marvelous birthday ever. She is truly alive." My family and friends express their delight, praising me, wishing Linda a happy birthday.

Susan and I, with Linda, watch two birthday videos together in the evening; one with Linda as an eight-year-old, the other on her 18th birthday when I sing "Happy Birthday" to her.

As I lie in bed that evening, overcome by the awe-inspiring joy of the day's events, Linda materializes, "I love you very much Dad for making it all possible."

# June 2014

On Pentecost Sunday, Susan and I attend Mass on Staten Island to celebrate seven-year-old Justin Robert's First Holy Communion. J.R. is a child with autism. Consequently, the priest, sensitive to this condition, makes an exception allowing J.R. to receive his communion apart from his classmates on Saturday. In the first row is my cousin Robert, his wife Natalie, their twin daughters Lauren and Ashley, Uncle Bob, and Natalie's mother Arlene.

I discern my Aunt Marion appear facing J.R., stroking the hair on his head. Adjoining her, Grandma Tessy is sitting in front of J.R., Aunt Joanne to his left and Linda to his right.

When J.R., in his beautiful white communion suit, walks to the priest to receive the Host, the whole congregation applauds, a dry eye in the church cannot be found.

After receiving Holy Communion, I return to my pew, saying a prayer of thanksgiving. Linda articulates, "The Holy Spirit wants you to open your eyes." I am startled as to what I witness: a white dove descending over each person receiving communion, above each dove a tongue of fire. The Holy Spirit is showing me angelic beings blessing and guiding the communicants who receive the same tribute given to the apostles on that first Pentecost Sunday.

On Tuesday, June 10th, I am on Sanibel where my friend Frank and I ride our bikes to a secluded part of the island and follow a foot trail leading to a beach inhabited only by shells and gorgeous homes. At 1:15 PM, we are swimming in the Gulf of Mexico, about 20 yards from shore. All of a sudden, we are bombarded with a frenzy of flying fish that hit us in the face, head, arms, and legs. Frank turns, viewing a huge disturbance in the gulf some 50 yards behind us, and yells "Get out. Something is wrong!" As we ride back to the condo, I ask Linda, "Why did you make those fish hit us?"

That evening, my friend Doug calls to confirm our boat outing for the following day. He asks, "Did you hear what happened today? A 14-foot Great White shark named Katherine was spotted via satellite off the coast of Sanibel. It was tagged on August 9th, 2013, off Cape Cod; its progress has been monitored ever since."

When I tell Frank of my conversation with Doug, Frank affirms, "It is Linda who saves us. Your daughter always appears to me. What are the odds those fish would hit us? Five feet in either direction they would miss us completely. There is no one else in the ocean as far as the eye can see, no one to alert us.

"A great white can swim in four feet of water. I'm a fisherman and boat on open waters. I've seen shark feeding frenzies and this is one, whether it is Katherine or another shark."

Linda sends those fish in our direction, but I let Frank acknowledge it. (When I return home, I go online, investigate Katherine, and she is recorded pinging off the coast of Sanibel on June 10th, 2014, at 8:14 AM, and again at 3:34 PM.)

On Wednesday, we boat to Cabbage Key for lunch. The dollar bill that reads "LINDA IS MY GAL," is still dangling above the table, over one year since my cousin Charlie spots it. And yes, my dollar bill with Linda's name on it is still taped tightly to the wall.

On Sunday, June 15th, while waiting to board Jet Blue Flight 930 back to JFK, total strangers wish me a happy Father's Day. During the flight, sitting in 16C, an aisle seat, I ask for a bag of pretzels which taste very salty. I whisper, "Linda, I can really use a bottle of water right now."

As soon as I articulate this, I turn and in the opposite aisle seat, a woman holding up a bottle of water turns to call the flight attendant. Saying to her, "Is something wrong?" she replies, "Out of nowhere, this bottle rolled down the aisle and hit my foot." Laughing, I reply, "I'll take it if you don't mind. When I ask my daughter for something, she usually brings it right away."

By nighttime, I count 15 people whom I've never met, who wish me a happy Father's Day. Prior to bed, I read every Father's Day card Linda ever sent me, even the one with stickers of Minnie, Daisy, and Mickey – my day complete.

# What's It All About?

Over the years I have met many people who have the natural ability to access the non-physical. As young children, we all have the capability to shift freely between the physical and non-physical. The veil that blocks this access slowly forms as we mature.

♥♥♥

At 18 months old, Linda is sitting on the couch staring at something in the opposite direction. I ask her, "What are you looking at?" She replies, "Judy Garland." Her answer nearly knocks me over considering no one ever mentions Judy Garland beforehand. Linda is too young to watch *The Wizard of Oz*; old enough only for *Sesame Street* and the Disney cartoons *Mickey Mouse* and *Winnie the Pooh*. Linda's first movie in the theatre is *Snow White*, a surprise outing for her third birthday.

♥♥♥

Fortunately for some people, the veil never takes semblance. These people retain the natural ability to access the other side. Most are ordinary people like you and me. Some develop their abilities further by being guided on their journeys toward enlightenment.

In our circle of friends and family, many such *naturals* exist. Mostly we choose to shrug off what they say as coincidental, strange, or out there. This is just our egos, inner judges, insecurities, and survival instincts blocking that which is different. "Your mind is like a parachute. It works best when it's open."

We must permit ourselves to listen to those with these natural abilities, acknowledging the benefits they bring to us. They are delegates here to help us on our journey, to help us understand there is no separation.

Let their messages resonate within our hearts and lift the veil between the physical and non-physical. To them, accessing the other side is as commonplace as driving a car or riding a bike. They are people who guide us in reclaiming our birthright to communicate with the other side.

There are many, many people around us with these abilities. I introduce those with whom I have come in direct contact, whether by reading their books or attending their seminars. Even some of my patients possess these abilities.

Many choose to become psychics, healers, mediums, channelers, and writers of books. They also establish institutes where others can go "to find out for themselves," as Bob Monroe would say.

The Monroe Institute doesn't impose any dogma or religious philosophy. Its only credo is, "You are more than your physical body."

There are other centers available to explore and learn: The Omega Institute, The Diamond Heart, and Ramtha's School of Enlightenment to name just a few.

♥♥♥

Our individual paths are unique and the teachings we receive support them. Our higher selves assist us through inner guidance and the development of our souls on our spiritual journeys.

In the advancement of our spirituality, we learn to trust our personal process. We come to respect our own individual pathway and direction, knowing what is real, innate, and normal, honoring the same in others. Here is a simple example: We can all see the same movie, yet have different opinions of what we understand and comprehend. By sharing our interpretation with others, we make the experience more entertaining and enjoyable. Without judgment, we can love, respect, admire, and be interested in what the other person has to say, thus remaining friends agreeing to meet again.

♥♥♥

I revere those with natural abilities; i.e. psychics, mediums, etc. However, I needed to nurture these capacities on my own. Curiosity led me to teach myself, ask questions, and to persevere. The spiritual law–*Discipline through excellence leads to freedom*–guides me. This law applies to millions of us who want to do something, to strive to change ourselves and help others.

Growing up in Brooklyn, everyone played some kind of ball. With very little money, the street became our ballfield, bustling with talented ballplayers. I watched, I played, I learned. Improving through discipline resulted in invitations to play more and more, allowing me the freedom to participate and have fun.

Practicing long hours playing the guitar, the piano, running track, and doing impersonations eventually paid off, enabling me to be in a band, win medals, and go on stage. By studying hard every night, I was able to get good grades and attend excellent universities.

We must respect and honor our own abilities. We process information differently through our five senses. Some are better at hearing, or tasting, or smelling, or touching. Your dominant sense is what your loved ones will use to communicate with you.

Many people remark if you can't see a soul once they transform, then they aren't alive. You may have a "sensation" they are standing next to you, or may smell their perfume, cologne, cooking, or brand of cigar they smoked while they were "here." Their favorite song may come on as soon as you think of them, or you may ponder a flower that reminds you of their favorite color. Some of us will even have the hairs on our arms or back of our neck stand up on end when they brush by us.

How many times have their pictures moved, books they enjoyed fallen off a shelf, numbers they played or coins appeared out of nowhere just to get your attention? Even just talking about them means they are alive. Writing helps to confirm your knowing. Reading in your own handwriting what transpires in your daily connection with them brings validation.

But most important, our children and loved ones can inhabit our bodies and intermingle with us. We need to cultivate our own innate abilities and become aware of their presence–it can be very subtle. Learning to become sensitive to these subtle events by quieting ourselves allows precious experiences to take place. Be open, for example, to re-embracing the initial movements of tiny hands and feet in the womb; reliving the moments you held and gazed into the eyes of your child or loved one for the first time, initiating their return into your arms again.

♥♥♥

Our written and spoken language, our concept of time and space, our thoughts, actions, and belief systems define who we are. The conscious mind views reality arbitrarily measured in seconds, minutes, hours, days, weeks, months, and years, manipulating it to conform to our needs: Daylight Savings Time, Leap Year. The clock, an integral part of processing our existence and how we function, doesn't apply on the other side.

We acknowledge ourselves via our positions in society, our professions, our daily routines; the size of our homes, the cars we drive, our seat at the dinner table, our height and weight. These tangibles are illusions of this realm, not valid in the celestial.

Our children who make their transition before us, define who we are. Their courage in fulfilling their agreement to transition prior to our own transition paves the way for our soul's journey. Being aware of their gifts, guidance, and interactions with us, we are compelled to a higher evolution. In doing so, we honor the sacrifices they undertake for us.

Because of this, our destinies are altered. The unnatural membrane that prevents us from accessing the other side is removed. They are our angels, our spiritual guides, entrusted to our care. They are sent to us by God so we can live beyond our temporal attachments allowing us to awaken to the limitlessness of our spiritual nature. We are chosen to be their parents, and bow to them, praising their undeniable devotedness and the lessons they teach.

♥♥♥

As human beings, we need hard, definitive, cognitive proof of something before we accept it as unquestionable, run-of-the-mill conventional. The Earth, over five billion years old, is a planet whose north-south dimensions are 40 miles longer than its equatorial latitude, pretty much a symmetrical sphere. Not until March

1493, when Columbus returned to Lisbon, Portugal, did humanity comprehend the Earth as round.

When Alexander Graham Bell uttered the first words to Mr. Watson, we grasped that sound was able to travel through a wire. Thomas Edison illuminated our lives forever with the first successful light bulb. It took the Wright brothers to show that man can indeed fly in a heavier-than-air machine. Einstein, in the publication of several papers in 1915, proved that light can be bent and the space-time continuum altered. The light we see from the North Star, Polaris, emanating 323 light years in the past is perceived by us in the present. Yet, this light exists in another juncture of time and space when it reaches us.

We are a society that relies heavily on statistics as proof in defining who we are. The current population on Earth is seven billion, and the total population since the beginning of recorded history is 108 billion. *If every person knows only one other person who has a real, verifiable experience with a loved one who transitions, the numbers become staggering.* Given these numbers along with the facts presented in this book and my confirmable interactions with Linda and others in the non-physical, we can no longer ignore the continuation of life beyond physical reality! It is here to stay!

I expound in unequivocal, common, daily, reproducible encounters, the uninterruption of existence, the verifiability of immortality, and the fact there is no separation, just a shift from one embodiment to the next.

I include with utmost humility and gratitude, those credible, courageous men and women preceding me, honoring their process and service to humanity, building upon their achievements, research, and results, in order to make this book possible. I also acknowledge those who shall come after me to continue the conscious exploration expounding further proof of the lifting of the shroud and the perpetuation beyond physicality.

In 2012, we were buzzing about the end of the Mayan calendar, the possibility of our mortality, and the changing of reality as we know it. Well, the Mayan calendar is correct.

An explosive awakening in consciousness has initiated an expansive recognition of institutes of learning, of how we view ourselves and the world around us through our ability to access books, movies, radio, television programing, and internet sites supporting this revelation.

In 2014, our modern forms of communication, (which may be obsolete in a few years), lead to changing definitions of words, thoughts, and actions. We Skype (video), FaceTime (the Jetson's cartoons of the 1960s), Instagram (take photos), selfie (photographs of ourselves), photobomb (Linda always sticks herself in photos at the last second), hashtag (renaming of the pound sign on our smart phones), Twitter (short texts), and download apps. I introduce the word *transition* to redefine one more term in our communication and thought processes, viz. death. *Transition is the lifting of the veil between the physical and non-physical, the rebirth, the transfiguration of the soul in the light.*

♥♥♥

*Linda in the Light* redefines the concepts of communication, time, and space as we comprehend them. Linda writes the book through me as our journeys intertwine. Therefore a near-death encounter isn't necessary in order to lift the veil accessing our essential birthright of everlasting life.

As I stated at the outset, I share what I learn through curiosity, exploration, courage, and participation and guidance from Linda. If you are open, your loved ones, your children can emerge through you, touching you in ways you never dreamed of; validating their presence, their existence in the beyond, bringing joy back to our lives. Once again, possessing no natural abilities, if I can learn how to experience this knowing of life eternal as real, natural, and normal, so can you!

As infants, we are showered with unconditional love; kissed, hugged, and cuddled from parents, grandparents, siblings, aunts, uncles, and friends, many of whom we don't remember who are long since gone. Yet, their beings are infused into our subconscious. They have passed on to us the continuation of life eternal, something we embody as we communicate with our children.

Picture yourself 100 feet in the air, looking down on your surroundings. What do you see?–you see yourself from a different vantage point, a different dimension, a different perspective, existing both on earth and from above; yet you are still you, alive.

That, my friends, is a simple way of viewing our children and loved ones; they are alive, existing in a different vantage point, a different dimension, a different perspective.

# It Continues with No Ending

Linda appears to me on three different occasions as a shadow silhouette. My curiosity leads me to search online for "shadow pictures of souls." As I am scrolling through the pictures, Linda cries out, "Stop! This is how I appear to you as an apparition. Let everyone see it."

*Linda's high school graduation party, 2003*

*Shadow apparition of Linda*

Verses from James Taylor's, "You've Got a Friend," depict Linda's existence on all levels:

When you're down and troubled and you need a helping hand
and nothing, whoa, nothing is going right
Close your eyes and think of me and soon I will be there
to brighten up even your darkest night–
When the skies above you become dark and full of clouds
keep your head together and call my name out loud,
Soon I will be knocking at your door–
You just call out my name, and you know wherever I am
I'll come running to see you again
Winter, spring, summer, or fall, all you have to do is call, Lord, I'll be there,
yeah, yeah
you've got a friend
Ain't it good to know you've got a friend
Oh, yeah, yeah, you've got a friend

♥♥♥

. . . ONE MORNING DURING AN OBE, LINDA ENUNCIATES, "DAD, WRITING THIS BOOK KEEPS ME ALIVE. IT IS VERY IMPORTANT TO LET PEOPLE KNOW THEY DON'T HAVE TO WAIT UNTIL ILLNESS OR TRAGEDY COME INTO THEIR LIVES TO REACH OUT TO US. TALKING ABOUT LOVED ONES IS A BEAUTIFUL WAY TO KEEP US ANIMATE. EVERYONE CAN DO THIS AND IT MAKES US HAPPY. SHOW THEM WHAT YOUR MOTHER DOES TO KEEP HER FATHER ALIVE." . . .

Almost every night during dinner, when my sisters Connie, Terry, and I were young, my mother told us about our grandfather Charles, who made his transition before we were all born. We couldn't wait for dinner; my grandfather sitting next to us while we ate.

My mother was in the hospital for three of her first five years, not interacting much with my grandmother Mamie, who crossed over when my mother was five. So my grandfather, along with my Aunt Josie, were everything to my mother, my Uncle Sal, and Aunt Marianne.

Through her stories, we knew my grandfather: how he raised his children, what jobs he had to work, how they lost their house during the depression, having to live in a three-room apartment with no door separating them from the landlord downstairs. We felt what he felt, saw what he saw, knowing his unwavering devotion toward his children, never remarrying.

We experienced his handling my mother's sicknesses, my aunt's surgeries, and my uncle going off to the war in the Pacific. She read us letters my grandfather wrote to my uncle overseas, revealing his sensitivity and adulation regarding his children. She described him staying up many a night, after everyone was asleep, helping her finish school projects so she wouldn't fall behind. My grandfather is viable due to my mother's indulgence to us.

She told us much about Aunt Josie: how she cooked, cleaned, and held the family together, serving as a surrogate mother. She also shared as much as she could remember about Grandma Mamie.

We later shared these stories of Charles, Josie, and Mamie with my sister Marianne, who is almost 15 years younger than me. She didn't remember my mother too well because my mother's illnesses returned when Marianne was just a toddler. We all took turns raising her and going to work, while my father fought to keep my mother alive. He left his job to care for my mother night and day during the last six months of her life.

♥♥♥

Since her rebirth, Linda makes herself available to many of my family, friends, and patients. One Saturday afternoon in May 2014, Susan and I attend Terry's daughter Marisa's high school play, *Bye Bye Birdie*. Marisa has the role of Kim.

As she is singing, Linda and Terry appear beside us shedding tears of joy, and I begin crying too. Marisa's voice is simply angelic; the sound of which resonates not only in Susan's and my hearts, but Linda's and Terry's as well.

Linda is often next to me, helping me treat my patients. I treat a woman named Catherine, who is born blind. She transcribes books into braille and invites my staff and me at a previous date to observe her computers and software, showing us the actual process of transcribing books. She knew Linda well.

While I am treating Catherine, she explains to me she can't access her startup screen on the main computer that does the transcribing. She expresses concern over this, considering it will be days until a computer specialist is available, and the cost to repair or replace is quite steep. I suggest at the end of our visit, "Ask Linda, she is more than willing to help you."

When she returns to my office the following week, Catherine affirms, "Guess what?" I giggle, "Try me." She continues, "That night at home, I ask Linda for help. Linda whispers, 'You have the instruction manual for your main computer on another computer in your apartment and have forgotten about it since it was a long time ago. There you will find how to fix the startup screen.'"

On the Thursday preceding the July 4th weekend in 2014, Jenna, my office manager, to whom Linda appears quite often, tells me she ended a five-year relationship with a man she thought she would marry. She is emotionally distraught, spending most of the day crying.

That evening before she leaves, she laments, "How long can I take this pain." I suggest to her, "Talk to Linda. You'll meet a man who'll say, 'I am sent to you by Frank's daughter.'" I smile and wink at Jenna.

Jenna bursts into the office on Monday stating, "When I arrive home on Thursday evening, I pray to Linda, 'I haven't seen you for a while. I miss talking to you. Please help me. I don't deserve this.' I reluctantly go to a barbeque on July 4th. While I am there, I receive a text from a man named Joe. I met him when I was 17 and haven't spoken to him in years.

"He writes, 'I always think about you. I'm going to watch the fireworks at Coney Island tonight. Why don't you join me?' When I meet him that evening he has no idea I just ended my relationship. We speak for hours on end. Doc, I have to thank Linda for making this possible."

♥♥♥

Linda keeps other psychics and mediums busy. I receive a call from my cousin Donna in Palm Harbor, Florida. She is one of the *naturals* I mention earlier. She goes to a local psychic who discloses, "A girl named Linda is next to you and is always with you. She is trying to help you, to tell you to enjoy yourself."

A woman walks into the bank on Staten Island where my cousin Robert sells insurance, introducing herself as a medium. (At a subsequent meeting, she admits to Robert she has many celebrity clients, including an ABC morning talk show host.) She stands at his desk asserting, "You were out to dinner with a few people last night." Robert retorts, "Yes, I was."

She continues, "One person, a cousin named Joseph is there. He loves you very much. Another cousin, [referring to me] is there who recently lost a child. She wants him to know she's very happy. She watches over you and your children all the time."

♥♥♥

Linda and I are twin souls, incarnated in the same life cycle, something extremely rare when not born as identical twins. We exist simultaneously in both realities, knowing no separation.

In my many OBE's with Linda, a celestial in the highest vibration, she constantly works with young children during their crossing, bringing them into the angelic, assisted by my sister Terry, who spends her earthly years as a pre-school teacher. Together they create fairy tale adventures, play lands, amusement parks, zoos, and parties where these angels revel basking in their heavenly absoluteness.

I am blessed by this, but I miss Linda continually. I live my live for us both more fully and freely, comforted that our reunion in the divine shall be a joyous one. I have no fear in leaving, in transitioning.

I acknowledge Linda's courage and sacrifice in this lifetime with gratitude and humility. My gift is also your gift, which we receive when our children enter the radiance of eternity so our hearts, our souls, can experience the unending continuum of life.

*Linda and me celebrating my 50th birthday*

As a father, I pine seeking her definitive essence. Is there ever really a sunny day after the loss of a child? Emptiness constantly remains and I never start or end a day without weeping, without mourning. Parts of the song, "All The Things You Are," by Barbra Streisand, pretty much sum up the humanness in my longing:

Time and again I long for adventure

Something to make my heart beat the faster

What did I long for I never really knew

Finding your love I found my adventure

Touching your hand my heart beats the faster

All that I want in all of this world is—

You are the promised kiss of springtime

That makes the lonely winter seem long

You are the breathless hush of evening

That trembles on the brink

Of a lovely song

You are the angel glow that lights a star

The dearest things I've known are what you are

Someday my happy arms will hold you

And someday I'll know that moment divine

When all the things you are, are mine

♥♥♥

On Wednesday, March 5th, 2014, Susan and I meet up with my friends Darlene and Pete, his daughter Amanda, son-in-law Danny, and four-year-old granddaughter Haley at Disneyland in California. Pete and his wife Darlene are special friends to Linda.

Before I meet Susan, while living in New Jersey, Linda, Pete, Darlene, and I attend many sporting events. Darlene, a charming, unassuming woman, befriends many players and coaches. At Yankee Stadium, she takes Linda down to the field to talk with Derek Jeter and Mariano Rivera, and at Madison Square Garden, she accompanies Linda on the hardwood court to stand with Patrick Ewing.

When Pete and Darlene move to California, Linda and I visit them often; the girls doing their thing in Burbank, Hollywood, and Malibu. Inevitably Darlene strikes up a conversation with an actor or actress, chatting in a matter-of-fact manner, as Linda stands by, sometimes joining in herself. We all jokingly call Darlene the "Star Magnet." Pete and Darlene's unyielding affection towards Linda and their generosity brings Linda many hours of joy as she struggles with her ailments.

So it is only fitting their granddaughter Haley, whom I nickname, "Haley the Comet," gives me a wonderful memento in Disneyland.

While we are waiting on line for Toy Story 3D, she keeps us busy during the 45-minute line by playing tag, making the wait fun. When is waiting in line in Disneyland ever pleasurable?

As we board our seats, she demands, "Frank, I want to ride with you." I am shocked because I met Haley only once prior, at her baptism as an infant.

During our escapade, I notice her becoming frustrated by not being able to hit all of the 3D targets, but I don't want to interfere. Linda appears to me and points, "She wants your help. Go ahead and play with her like you play with me."

So, sliding my hands on her control wheel guiding her aim, Haley hits the targets and is now an effervescent ball of enthusiasm. We are shouting, cheering; carrying on as two kids are supposed to on a Disney animated ride. When we exit the ride, I exclaim to Haley, "You won 33,000 points!" She runs over to her parents, unable to contain her excitement.

As we walk to the next ride, Haley runs up to me and holds my hand. I discover overwhelming contentment, the beauty of pure, innocent tenderness only a child without an overlay can express. Her tiny, soft hand, her loving touch, the beauty of all that is good and precious in this world, are given to me through Haley; two individuals walking side by side, sharing a glorious moment.

My heart becomes enraptured and Linda expounds, "Your kindness to others allows you to receive what is important to all, pure joy and unconditional love! You walk in both dimensions and I am with you forever." Tears of happiness roll down my cheeks as I express to Linda, "Thank you for bringing Haley to me. You will always be within me, guiding me with gentleness."

♥♥♥

Linda constantly reminds Susan and me of her actuality. I am always followed by butterflies and Susan by two cardinals. Whether sitting in the screened-in porch, riding my bike, or meandering through our village; beautiful, large, colorful butterflies manifest and hover over me. The cardinals accompany Susan when she is gardening or delivering the mail. "Every day since her transition," Susan amazes, "Linda sends the cardinals to me."

♥♥♥

I know what I write resonates in your soul. Your insight is my insight, too. Honor your loved ones, your children, acknowledging their courage and undertaking. They fulfill their mission and we have to fulfill ours. Be amenable to the lifting of the veil: change your course, alter your destiny, keep your promise.

You possess the courage to make the journey. Follow your individual path, trust your higher self for guidance, respect your process allowing the beauty of creation into your heart. Do not dismiss the ordinary communication your children and loved ones want to share with you.

Once again, our children have given their lives so we can be exonerated from the attachments of the Earth Life System and ascend into the celestial just as they have.

Communication with them is real, natural, and normal; just as real, natural, and normal as when we first hold our children, experiencing the true knowing of unconditional enchantment, happiness, and joy.

As I glance down at the monitor on my computer, I notice the date, July 20th, 2014. Linda reminds me, "This is an important date in history." For thousands of years humanity anticipates this significant event. The simple words spoken 238,900 miles away from Earth–*That's one small step for man, one giant leap for mankind*–are relevant to my humble intent in writing the book, *Linda in the Light;* hoping that this effort provides but a single step into the reality of the continuance and perpetuity of the eternal.

♥♥♥

During the finalization of *Linda in the Light,* a few very unique events occur above and beyond my everyday interactions with Linda, and the book would not be complete without my sharing them.

For over six months, world-renowned medium and author, Jackie Barrett, had been suffering with earaches and spasms on the right side of her face, having to cancel several speaking engagements. Over this period she sought medical attention from various ear, nose, and throat specialists, and several dentists. No one could discover the cause of her discomfort.

During these six months, on her daily walks she would pass by my office where a young woman would constantly wave to her, asking her to cross the street. Jackie, since childhood, is able to discern between entities on the other side as vividly as those in their human embodiment.

Finally, the Sunday prior to Columbus Day, 2014, while taking one of her morning strolls, she is in so much discomfort she traverses the boulevard and sits down on the front steps of my office next to this woman who has been waving her over for months.

Jackie listens as the woman speaks, "You are in pain but shall be okay. This is the office where you will be treated. Frank will be in tomorrow to take care of you."

As Jackie remains resting on my steps, the wife of one of my colleagues recognizes her and approaches, "My husband practices across the street and he will open the office to help you." Jackie answers, "I am told by this young woman Frank will be in tomorrow to take care of me." My friend's wife seeing no one except Jackie, replies with a puzzling stare, "Tomorrow is a holiday and Frank won't be in." Jackie continues, "That's okay. I'll stay here and wait a while."

On Monday I am in my office treating patients. Jackie registers as an emergency, and with one digital radiograph and a simple palpation of the area, I diagnose and treat her problem, and her affliction is gone.

During the procedure, Jackie sees a child sitting behind me to her left side. Swinging her legs, wearing brown sandals on her feet, and pointing, she declares, "That's my Daddy." When I finish the procedure, during which I do a few Robert De Niro impersonations, Jackie reiterates her entire ordeal over the last six months up to the present moment. I show Jackie a picture of Linda as an adult on my iPhone. Jackie exclaims, "This is the woman who's been waving to me over the last six months!"

Linda often visits Jackie's house helping her treat clients and playing with her dog Violet. Jackie asserts, "Your daughter is so amazing; only the most advanced souls are amongst animals. She is constantly comforting young children who cross over guiding them in the light."

Linda even saves Jackie from an explosion in her basement. One evening Jackie hears a voice downstairs. When she enters the basement, she notices a broken pipe, water on the floor, the gas water heater pilot out, but no odor in the air. Linda points a finger to the pilot yelling, "Shut of your gas valve. Call a plumber, now!"

In November 2014, I attend a second week-long Starlines II seminar at TMI. My good friends Franceen and Lee, along with a new trainer, Andrea Berger, are the facilitators for this program.

On the morning of Monday, November 17th, when I arise, I gaze at my collage of Linda and my other friends and family members who transition, and begin my morning meditation. Immediately I am overcome with the same agony and suffering–physically, emotionally, and psychologically–as on May 7th, 2012.

Thinking I would never have to entertain this sick and despondent feeling again, I slump to the floor, enthralled in despair, anguish, and bereavement. I can't identify the fields and the Blue Ridge Mountains from my window because my eyes are so full of tears.

My cries bellow from my gut, my heart rips open. "Why, why, why!" I bemoan lamenting to Linda, "You have given me so much since your transition. If I can only hold you once more." It's every parent's outcry when their child leaves. After an hour, I compose myself as best I can and join my colleagues.

At 10:30 AM during our second voyage through interdimensional travel, Linda sits beside me as part of our 20 member group. "I'm here with you Dad." I reach over, grab her, hug and kiss her. "It is really actually me. Feel me. See me. Hold me. Smell me. Laugh with me. I am alive sitting here. This is what you asked for this morning and why you are here this week. True love does transcend time and space."

I am beyond ecstatic! Creation in all its wonderment and glory. I burst forth in jubilation, experiencing exhilaration, euphoria, and rhapsody. I am captivated; simply blown-away! Father and daughter together once again; exploring, reaching, travelling.

"I will show you how we will appear when you transition," she proclaims. Linda and I join as a column of glittering, sparkling luminosity as eternal incarnates, untethered via chronology, space, or dimension.

Later on at our debriefing, many participants acknowledge the appearance of a young girl next to me during our exploration. I make no mention of Linda to anyone.

That evening I speak to Franceen, Lee, and Andrea of this event. I have so much energy, sleep is not an option that night. I indulge in the radiance of a miracle, thanking Linda and God for allowing such a wondrous benediction!

On the last day of the program, I enlighten the group by sharing my special encounter with Linda.

♥♥♥

I find going back and re-reading a book or viewing a movie for a second or third time is invaluable because you miss so much the first time around. I always remark, "Did they slip something in that wasn't there before?"

It's just that your perspective shifts; you become aware of messages that were there but you weren't ready to receive or understand them. *Linda in the Light* is this kind of book.

# With Gratitude

I am blessed to be surrounded by so many enlightened souls during my earthly sojourn. My guidance has honored me and I bow in homage and gratitude to those who accompany me on my journey.

One of my earliest spiritual guides who walks in the light is my former 6th grade teacher, Sister Flora Marinelli. At a youthful 81 years of age, she is the "Mother Teresa" of Long Island City, N.Y., bringing God's word to all religions, races, and creeds, abounding in absolute enlightenment, encompassing compassion and grace.

Karen Malik, a soul blessed with the essential qualities of wisdom, knowledge, guidance, and pure unconditional love, is a very, very, dear and special friend. Her unyielding support and insight during our long journey together kept me inspired and focused, allowing me to fulfill my promise to Linda in writing this book. She devotes her life so selflessly to conscious expansion and the evolution of the higher self. Her years of service are appreciated by all of us who attend TMI.

Karen holds a Master's degree in Clinical Psychology and she is a Senior Fellow with the Biofeedback Certification Institute of America. She has served on the board and is past president and conference chairperson of the International

Society for the Study of Subtle Energies and Energy Medicine.

Dr. Franceen King, a close friend and part of the incredible guidance team at TMI, has done so much to bring into consciousness the reality of non-physical realms. Part of Bob Monroe's original team, along with Karen Malik, she paves the way for us all to know better our Total Selves and achieve our higher purposes.

Franceen holds both a Master's Degree in Community Mental Health Counseling and a Ph.D. in Clinical Sexology. My unyielding gratitude and love to her for who she is and what she represents to us all.

Lee Stone, the ultimate time traveler, has opened doorways for me that I never dreamed were possible. A longtime friend from TMI, as are Karen and Franceen, Lee has been instrumental in my communication with Linda as real, normal, and everyday matter-of-fact.

He is nationally certified in Neuro-Linguistic Programming Psychotherapy and Clinical Hypnotherapy with the International Association of Counselors and Therapists. He has an extensive background in Buddhist Vipassana Meditation, Energy and Multidimensional Healing, and is an Usui Reiki Master. Also an internationally-collected artist, Lee has paintings that can be found in public and private galleries in twenty-four countries.

My heartfelt appreciation goes out to my fellow participants over the years and to the entire team at TMI: Laurie Monroe, (who made her transition in 2006), Rosalind McKnight (who made her transition in 2010), Carol de la Herrán (who made her transition in 2013), Andrea Berger, Joe and Nancy "Scooter" McMoneagle, Darlene Miller, F. Holmes "Skip" Atwater, Angie, Tammy, and of course Carolyn.

But most importantly, I am forever indebted to that great man, who had a vision to establish a place where people can *"go and find out for themselves,"* Bob Monroe, my guide, my teacher, my mentor, my messenger in my OBE adventures.

Robert Allan Monroe founded The Monroe Institute, currently located in Faber, Virginia, in 1971. A successful radio and television producer during the 1950s, Bob did research in sound pattern technologies, later patented as Hemi-Sync, and began having out-of-body experiences (OBEs) in 1958.

Seeing there was no center dedicated to the exploration of expansion of human potential, this man of extraordinary insight, conviction, courage, and curiosity, created an institute to further advance the study of what we have come to know today as natural and commonplace.

He wrote three books, *Journeys Out of the Body* (1971), *Far Journeys* (1985), and *Ultimate Journey* (1994), which have been read by millions of people throughout the world. His legacy continues today in outreach centers around the globe, guided by his simple credo, *"You are more than your physical body."*

Bob Monroe is my eternal friend. I love and respect him for all he has made possible for me and others who travel the path of enlightenment. Without him, Linda, Jeannie Callahan, and the others throughout this book, there would be no *Linda in the Light.*

Jeannie Callahan, the gifted channeler, healer, psychic, Reiki Master, and medium sent to me by Linda, is most instrumental to the writing of this book. Allowing Linda to inhabit her being, she became a vessel through which actual, indisputable truths were revealed, proving to all, without a shadow of doubt, the lifting of the veil between the physical and non-physical, the confirmation of life eternal; allowing us to experience the gifts our children and loved ones came here to bestow upon us.

Jeannie is on her own journey with her book *"Disguised Blessings,"* a journey which I am honored to be part of. She exudes all that is good in humanity, all that is encompassing in spirituality, and all that reverberates in the light on the other side.

I extend my thanks to world-renowned medium and author, Jackie Barrett.

Brought to my office by Linda on Columbus Day, 2014, Jackie made sure my voice was heard by over 47 million people before the publishing of *Linda in the Light*.

Harriette McDonough, also sent to me by Linda after Linda's transition, played a key role in allowing new energy patterns to be brought to the forefront of my consciousness, freeing me to move to a higher vibration.

She is a New York State Licensed Master of Social Work and a Diplomate of Comprehensive Energy Psychology.

Dr. Nicholas Fargnoli, my next-door neighbor and great friend, holds a Ph.D. in Theology and English Literature, is Dean of Humanities at Molloy College in Rockville Centre, N.Y., and President of The James Joyce Society. Along with his wife Harriett, who has a Master's Degree in Library Science, Nick offered invaluable comments, suggestions, and encouragement. They read (and listened to) several versions of the book as it was taking shape, and unselfishly donated their time and expertise. Linda giggles as I write this, whispering in my ear, "Nothing is by chance!"

Francis Bonnet, a graduate with a degree in Illustration from the Fashion Institute of Technology in New York, has used his talents, skills, and abilities to create the cover, formatting, and text design for *Linda in the Light* as well as the website www.lindainthelight.com. His countless hours and tireless efforts are greatly appreciated. He has his own comic strip, *Suburban Fairy Tales*, and is part of the administrative staff at Molloy College.

Special gratitude is bestowed upon Dr. Michael S. Russo, Professor of Philosophy at Molloy College, founder of SophiaOmni Press and Ars Omnia Press. His invaluable assistance, commitment, and generous time were crucial in orchestrating and bringing to fruition the publication of this book. His endeavors are why you are reading *Linda in the Light* today.

Logistically, everyone needs an excellent IT organization in your armamentarium to work out the temperamental nature of a desktop, laptop, tablet, or smart phone. David Streit, lifelong friend, and Principal of Stephill Associates, LLC, was always there: answering my calls and remedying unforeseen issues with the kind heart, patience, and skill only someone like he possesses in the ever-changing field of computer technology.

I am lucky to be blessed with many best friends and family members who supported me during the writing of *Linda in the Light.* My heartfelt gratitude to Sanibel Mike Conti, Dr. Frank Colabella, Judy Reddington, Ann Marie Pagnotta, my sisters Connie Telesco and Marianne La Batto, and my cousins Angela Ritchie, Charlie Calta, Roe and Patricia Caleca, Donna La Batto, Robert Paventi and his son Justin Robert.

One of my great buddies, Douglas Winthrop, who lost his sight due to retinitis pigmentosa and reads by audio books only, suggested my reading the manuscript out loud and then playing it back to hear what it really sounds like. This proved to be an invaluable tool and brought great insight as to the flow and energy of this book.

I bow in homage to all of my family and friends who send guidance to me through their transitioning, especially my sister, Terry. Her unyielding support and unconditional love for Linda, both during their earthly embodiment together and their sojourn in the light, bring this book to the highest celestial vibration.

Where would I be today without my loving wife Susan. Patient, kind, gentle, understanding, and oh, so supportive, she spent many a night waiting up for me as I wrote and wrote and wrote, easing my frustrations with a simple kiss, hug, and excellent Italian cooking.

And lastly, Linda–sweet, adorable, lovely Linda–whom I love so very, very much; sent to me by God, my twin soul, holding my hand, sitting next to me, guiding my fingers on the keyboard, writing through me as our journeys throughout eternity intertwine. I honor all of her lifetimes and the lessons they teach.

I write this book in homage to her and to all of us who have been fortunate to be given the responsibility to care for little angels who go by so many, many, many faces and names, who bring true joy to our hearts, pure unconditional love to our lives, happiness to our inner beings, and lessons for us to learn.

We are the lucky ones to be given the chance to see, feel, hear, touch, and understand the timeless and limitless possibilities in the light, the glory of creation. Life eternal is just a simple vibration separating this side from the other.

It is a gift available to us all!

# Glossary

Feel free to add to this list and research any topic, author, or term used in *Linda in the Light* to assist you on your individual journey, your individual knowing, your individual experiences with your children and loved ones in the light.

**Carnal**    Term used to define anything relating to the physical body.

**Celestial**    Word used describing or suggesting heaven or divinity.

**Chakras**    A Chakra is a main energy center, a wheel-like spinning vortex connected to a major organ or gland. Along the spinal cord there are seven main Chakra centers.

**Channeled**    The direct result of communication between a physical person and non-physical being.

**Channeler**    A channeler is a person who conveys thoughts, energy, feelings, and sounds outside of the their own body or conscious mind. They speak and interact directly with non-physical beings.

**Earth Life Cycle**  The physical time spent on Earth from birth to transition. This cycle is repeated until all of our lessons in physical reality are learned.

**Earth Life System**  The organized area of time-space that we inhabit on Earth. Eventually we graduate from this system and move to other, more advanced physical and non-physical realms.

**EFT Method of Healing**  Commonly called the Emotional Freedom Technique, it is a method of emotional clearing by utilizing 14 Meridian Points which are centers (areas) on the body containing major energy release points.

**Ego**  One's individual identity–the identity by which someone knows him or herself and has a sense of self as separate from others.

**Endorphins**  Any group of substances found in the central nervous system, especially the brain, that when released, create a healing or euphoric effect, reducing physical pain and emotional suffering.

**Essential Birthright**  Because we are spiritual beings in human existence, we possess at our core the perfect manifestation of God within us. It is our birthright to recognize, develop, and nurture this manifestation of who we are as spiritual beings, as we progress towards achieving enlightenment while on Earth.

**Ethereal**  Relating to anything spiritual or heavenly.

**Higher Selves or Self**    It is the source of our inner wisdom and guidance. It guides us through an optimizing force and loving intelligence concerning all things. It knows our *plan* for this current physical life, and escorts us toward fulfilling our spiritual journey while on Earth.

**Incarnation**    Also referred to as reincarnation, simply stated, depicts the act of the soul becoming human lifetime after lifetime to evolve in wisdom and eventually reach the point where it no longer has to manifest itself in physical form.

**Lifeline Program**    Lifeline is a unique and powerful program developed by The Monroe Institute that takes you into profound states of consciousness using Hemi-Sync audio-guidance technology.  The participants learn to explore Focus Levels 23-27, specific states of awareness associated with the afterlife state. They discover how to enter into these states of consciousness, comfortably make contact with people who have passed over, perform "rescues and retrievals," and return at will.  In addition, techniques to direct healing energies to those still in physical embodiment are developed.

**Lower Selves or Self**    The instinctual, emotional, unconscious, animal self that governs human nature and the survival drive. It is the combination of the soul and the physical body together and is responsible for our material wants in this reality. Surpassing these antiquated qualities allows for spiritual development and maturation of our soul.

**Medium**    A medium is a person who acts as an intermediary between physical and non-physical reality, has fine-tuned his or her extrasensory perception and can interface with souls in other dimensions. Mediums are able to become completely receptive to the higher frequency or energies and feel, hear, and translate when entering an expanded state of awareness.

**Metaphysical**    A term used to describe a type of philosophy or study that uses broad concepts to help define reality and our understanding of it. This discipline generally seeks to explain inherent or universal elements which are not easily discovered or experienced in our everyday life. As such, it is concerned with explaining the features of reality that exist beyond the physical world and our immediate senses. This includes but is not limited to: spirituality, higher self, simultaneous parallel lifetimes, the nature of the human mind, the definition and meaning of existence, and the study of space-time or absence thereof.

**Near-Death Experience**    A near-death experience (NDE) refers to a personal experience associated with impending death, encompassing multiple possible sensations including detachment from the body, feelings of levitation, total serenity, security, warmth, the experience of absolute dissolution, and the presence of a light; interactions with divine entities and family members and friends who have transitioned. These experiences are usually reported after an individual has been pronounced clinically dead or has been very close to death and has returned to physical consciousness.

**OBE or Out-of-Body Experience**    An experience that involves the separation and dissociation of oneself from one's physical body; viewing oneself from an external perspective. An OBE can occur spontaneously or through meditation. It is in this state that one can travel to other dimensions and realities, communicate and interact with others who are no longer physical, experiencing everything as if one is in the present moment. All manners of touch, taste, sight, sound, environment, emotion, feeling, action, and thought are as real as in the conscious state.

**Other Side**     The dimension of no time or space beyond physical Earth often called the spiritual realm.

**Paramount**     Of the highest ranking; supreme; most important.

**Reiki Master**     Reiki is a form of therapy that uses simple hands-on or no-touch, and visualization techniques, with the goal of improving the flow of life energy in a person. The basic concept underlying reiki is that the body has an energy field that is central to its health and proper functioning, and this energy travels in certain pathways that can become blocked or weakened. After undergoing a series of attunements (training sessions) in Reiki I and II, the student attains the highest level of attunement and becomes a Reiki Master. It is at this level the master attains the potential to heal virtually all illness, transferring unlimited love, joy, peace, compassion, wisdom, and abundance.

**Somatic**     Pertaining to the physical body and the stimulus that interacts with the body, i.e., touch, taste, sound, heat, vibration, etc.

**Soul**     The spiritual part of humans, as distinct from the physical part, that separates from the body and survives after the transition from the Earth Life Cycle, existing in the infinite. It is through the soul that one develops and matures in spirituality. It is malleable and therefore effected by life's experiences.

**Soul Retrievals**     A technique developed in the Lifeline Program which teaches the participants to make contact with those souls who have transitioned, yet still believe they are in human embodiment. These souls are often "stuck" and appear as ghosts to us in the physical. It is during this contact that the participants help the transitioned soul realize that they are no longer in their physical form and can ascend to a higher vibration. These retrievals take place in Focus 23, bringing the soul to Focus 27, as explained in the chapter entitled, "June 2012."

**Starlines II Program**     This program, developed by Dr. Franceen King at The Monroe Institute, is a blend of physics and metaphysics poised at the convergence of science, technology, and consciousness. Employing ultradeep Focus Level 49, Starlines II strengthens the energetic pathway between the earth core and the galactic core, giving the participants the opportunity to explore forms of emerging patterns of awareness and dimensional shifting; including teachings from cultures where space-time shifting is accepted and used. Building on these new understandings, the participants examine perspectives reminding them that they are not only more than their physical bodies; they are more than the physical universe, more than the infinite parallel universes that science hypothesizes.

**Super Ego**     One's *inner judge* that develops during childhood by internalizing the rules, morals, and values of our parental role models, authority figures, society, and religion.

**The Monroe Institute**     A center of conscious expansion and exploration established by Bob Monroe in 1971, whose headquarters are in Faber, Virginia, with outreach centers all over the world. To truly appreciate and understand what TMI has done to accelerate the development of mankind, kindly visit their website at www.monroeinstitute.org.

**Timeline Program**     This program, developed by Lee Stone at The Monroe Institute, works primarily in the state of no-time, Focus 15, guiding the participants step-by-step toward knowing their life's higher purpose, gaining new insights about how to live more fully. Timeline leads the participants first to revisit the early years of their current life, uncovering and releasing old beliefs or recurring emotions that have limited or obstructed progress. Next, they are guided into a deep exploration of *past lives*, other aspects of consciousness, toward a new understanding of the origins of current life situations; healing and releasing the past, creating an opening to a more purposeful and fulfilling future. Ultimately, led to move forward in local time, the participants meet their higher selves, perceiving *future events*, receiving clarity about their purpose, and gaining a new life overview.

**Transfiguration**     A complete change of form or appearance into a more beautiful or spiritual state; a divine act to exalt and glorify.

**Transformation**     The thorough or dramatic act of changing in form, shape, or appearance; the metamorphosis from one composition to another.

**Transition**     Transition is the lifting of the veil between the physical and non-physical, the rebirth, the transfiguration of the soul in the light.

# *About the Author*

Dr. Frank A. La Batto was born in Brooklyn, New York. After having his first out-of-body experience (OBE) at 18 years of age, he became curious, read books, attended many programs at The Monroe Institute, developed abilities in conscious expansion, rescued souls who transitioned to the other side, and worked on many levels in the non-physical. Though not being born with the natural gift of accessing the other side, he has become aware, through his personal life-journey, of the reality of the continuum of life on all planes of existence. The ability to access the other side as real and normal is a gift we all possess as part of our essential birthright and is readily available to all.

His training at NYU College of Arts and Sciences and NYU College of Dentistry led him to work with world famous prosthodontist, Dr. Maurice Saklad. Dr. La Batto assisted Dr. Saklad with many famous celebrities in the 1980s, including Frank Sinatra, Greta Garbo, Olivia Newton-John, Vice President Spiro T. Agnew, David Brenner, and Willie Mays.

Dr. La Batto then completed a two-year fellowship in Surgical Orthodontics at the Institute of Reconstructive Plastic Surgery at NYU Medical Center. Here he worked with children born with severe facial deformities, under the guidance of Dr. Barry Grayson and Dr. Joseph McCarthy. He published a paper in *The American Journal of Orthodontics* on Basilar Cephalometric Analysis.

Dr. La Batto developed a specialized practice in dentistry for 33 years in Bay Ridge, Brooklyn. Combining his training in dentistry with his devotion to conscious expansion and healing, he created a practice that treated patients of all ages who had extreme fear and anxiety and had been wounded by prior dental experiences. He intuitively understood that he worked in the sacred space between the Throat and Third Eye Chakras. This allowed him to not only heal the patient physically, but also work with the patient in healing past life imprints that manifested themselves in the human condition. Dr. La Batto knew the patients that sought him out were in need of more than just dental treatment.

Dr. La Batto volunteered for three years in the Child Life Clinic at Robert Wood Johnson University Hospital in New Jersey, not as a doctor, but as an everyday person doing what he does best: making children laugh, playing video games, giving out ice cream and candy, visiting those children too sick to get out of bed, and preparing their parents for the eventual transition their children would undertake.

Dr. La Batto has a variety of interests. He plays the piano, paints in oil, and does impersonations and comedy routines he began developing when he was 13 years old. He comes from a middle-class family and had to deal with the tragic loss of many family members at a very young age.

He held a variety of jobs growing up; paperboy, dishwasher, cashier, clothing salesman, working in a corrugated box factory, a travel agent with Circle Travel Service, and manager of McDonald's. He ran track in grammar school and high school winning many medals. He went back to give his time as a track coach to young children at his grammar school for many years.

Dr. La Batto most cherishes the time spent with Linda in the 27 years of her physical presence on Earth; experiencing and knowing the true love between a father and his daughter.

Linda made her transition on May 7th, 2012. He now engages with Linda in the non-physical–a relationship free from the distractions of human existence. Incarnated in the same Earth Life Cycle as twin souls, something very rare and sacred when not born as identical twins, Linda works with him in both the physical and non-physical as their journeys intertwine. Linda vibrates in the highest level in the light. She helps many people in the physical and many souls who have transitioned to the non-physical.

Dr. La Batto shares with us the experiences given to him by Linda and proves that the gifts our loved ones, especially our children, present to us are real, normal, and natural. They are our teachers, guides, and angels in the light. Our children want us to live, laugh, and love. By doing so, we honor the courage and sacrifice they made before entering this physical life. Pure unconditional love is what we are here to learn. It heals the tragedy, the wounds, the pain, the sadness, and the anger of the physical separation we all experience when we lose a child or loved one.

Dr. La Batto resides on Long Island with his wife, Susan, her daughter, Annie, and their two cats and one dog.

Please visit our website:

**www.lindainthelight.com**